At Home in Joshua Tree

A FIELD GUIDE TO DESERT LIVING

Sara and Rich Combs

Creators of the Joshua Tree House

RUNNING PRESS

PHILADELPHIA

Running Press
Hachette Book Group
1290 Avenue of the Americas, New York, NY 10104
www.runningpress.com
@Running_Press

Printed in China

First Edition: October 2018

Published by Running Press, an imprint of Perseus Books, LLC,
a subsidiary of Hachette Book Group, Inc. The Running Press name
and logo is a trademark of the Hachette Book Group.

The Hachette Speakers Bureau provides a wide range of
authors for speaking events. To find out more, go to
www.hachettespeakersbureau.com or call (866) 376-6591.
The publisher is not responsible for websites (or their content)
that are not owned by the publisher.

Print book cover and interior design by Ashley Todd

Library of Congress Control Number: 2018947196

ISBNs: 978-0-7624-9167-4 (hardcover), 978-0-7624-9166-7 (ebook)

RRD-S

10   9   8

Contents

 # Life in the Desert

"Slow down, enjoy the view." These are the words we read as we drove into Joshua Tree for the first time. Now after years of living here, they still hold true to the spirit of this place. Our time living here has not necessarily been about doing less, but slowing each moment down to enjoy the process. The simplest moments of each day have become the most precious; they're the ones that determine our happiness. Our lives in the desert consist of many ordinary moments that are also a part of life in the city: brewing a morning cup of coffee, taking a bath or shower, daydreaming, or enjoying a conversation with friends. The difference lies in how we do these things and how they connect to the small reminders that nature gives us throughout the day. These reminders are sometimes lost in the city, with the distraction of tall buildings and artificial lights.

Were we crazy never to notice before living here how dramatically the moon rises and sets on the horizon or how many stars appear without its presence? Did we not consider ourselves morning people because the sun wasn't visible from our bedroom window as it crept above the horizon? The sun now guides us through the experiences of each day—from early morning, when it gently nudges us awake, to the last bits of light that encourage us to get outside and enjoy the sunset. Removed from distraction in our home in the desert, we are intensely aware of the way the sun shifts across a room and the conversations held within. In the silence, we hear so much more. In the darkness, we see so much more. In turn, we have become like children again;

experiencing everything here in the desert as though we've never experienced it before. These simple moments, the ones we were always meant to notice but didn't, feel far more important than any possession we could ever own. As we continuously pare down our belongings, we're able to see what's truly important.

As you page through this book, you'll come across various design and decor ideas, thoughts on entertaining as a natural extension of home, light recipes, gardening advice, and mindful everyday practices to experience as the sun shifts across the sky. Our hope is that you can use this book as a guide to reconnect with the natural cycle of the sun and find liberation in appreciating the smallest moments of each day. Though it can take time to adjust, we hope that you find slowing down your daily rituals, and perhaps adding a few new ones, help you feel connected to your environment.

In the first part of this book you'll find the design mantras that we repeat to ourselves as we plan spaces that are meant to be lived in and experienced. After all, a home is nothing more than a geometrical space without the experiences held within it. These mantras are meant as a loose guide through a design process that considers much more than the aesthetics of a home, but how design has the ability to influence our daily routines. Just as our lives in the desert are guided by the sun, we've found it important for the design of our home to lead us through the day as well.

We've also reached out to some of our favorite desert lovers and dwellers to share their personal rituals and experiences, from sunrise to evening. Moroccan rug shop Soukie Modern, woodworker Aleksandra Zee, high desert restaurant La Copine, Casey Goch of Shreebs Coffee, beauty and wellness expert Tienlyn Jacobson, abstract painter Heather Day, painter Stella Maria Baer, Joshua Tree furniture studio Fire on the Mesa, painter Caris Reid, and herbalist Sophia Rose will be sharing

meditations, recipes, and other practices that encourage an understanding of ordinary moments as the most precious ones.

Finally, at the end of this book you'll find a guide filled with our favorite local shops, design resources, and places to source ingredients for the recipes we've included.

Our hope is that no matter where you live, this book will serve as a visual guide to designing a home that's not only beautiful, but enhances the enjoyment of everyday experiences in connection with the sun.

# How We Got Here

My childhood home had one large boulder out front, next to the road. That giant rock became my own personal wonderland. I'm reminded of the feeling of curiosity and liberation I experienced there as I'm now perched on a boulder in Joshua Tree, California, gathering my thoughts on what it has meant to live in our little corner of the Mojave Desert. It's fitting that my first thought as I climbed up this boulder was from childhood. In many ways, the desert has made me see the world with fresh eyes again, curious about the plants surrounding me, the changes each season will bring, and which animals I will get to know.

The high desert has a magnetic core at its center that gives many people a strong, unexplained desire to be in this place. We felt it after a one-night stay on a cross-country road trip, a strange feeling that no other place had previously given us. This magnetism is at the core of conversations we've had with many who have moved here or aspire to. It's difficult to put into words the comfort that the Joshua trees bring, the deep breath of the open horizon, the inspiration of the tough flora and fauna that call the desert home. Maybe it's that those who feel this pull crave the silence, to work with our hands, and to somehow revert back to simpler times. Or, maybe it's the flowing aquifers underneath the desert floor, and the quartz crystal in the rock formations here that simply radiate an inexplicable and addictive energy.

Our decision to move full-time to the Mojave all began with a road trip, as most major shifts in our lives have started. Movement and exploration always get our minds racing with new possibilities and open us up to people and ideas we otherwise wouldn't have known. After leaving our full-time jobs in 2013 to pursue life as freelance designers, we got in the car and drove from San Francisco to New York, stopping at as many national parks as we could find along the way. We would zoom in on Google Maps to places we'd never been or heard of before, and if the photos called to us, then off we went. Though we visited many beautiful places, Joshua Tree stood out from the rest and stayed in our thoughts.

We knew that somehow we wanted to be a part of this place, and so we set out to find a home. Now after living in Joshua Tree full-time for a couple of years, we're feeling more connected to nature than ever before. Joshua Tree is a place where the sun guides our day and wild animals are our neighbors. Rather than meeting up with friends at a bar or restaurant as we did in the city, in the desert we create our own entertainment. Our home has the ability to transform from a quiet morning meditation room to our own personal restaurant for brunch with friends or to the ultimate bohemian outdoor movie night. Indoor and outdoor spaces begin to blend together as we bring our favorite pieces outside and our favorite plants and rocks in.

We're often asked if we feel isolated or lonely living in the desert, but it's truly the reverse. We feel more connected now. Our small community is supportive, and we've found that people who come through town are in a more present state of mind for meaningful conversation. We end up going on hikes or having dinner parties at friends' houses rather than going out for dinners and shows. This is a place to create your own home, your own dreams—whatever they may be.

Sara and Rich Combs
JOSHUA TREE, CALIFORNIA

 # Design Mantras

As we have designed our own home, as well as spaces for others to gather, we've kept a few mantras close to heart. Each one began as an instinct, but over time we took note of patterns and design elements that made spaces feel particularly warm and full of love. The goal with these mantras is not perfection. Part of what makes a home comforting are the imperfections, the scars, and the stories.

We call these *mantras* because they're meant to be repeated as subtle reminders throughout the design process. As with meditation, if our mind wanders—and it will—it's incredibly helpful to have a key thought to refer back to that keeps us on our path. These mantras guide many small decisions into one cohesive design. As with most things, designing an entire home can feel daunting when imagining every detail at once. But when design is broken down into smaller decisions, guided by familiar daily routines within your home, the design process becomes much more comfortable.

When making decisions on materials to use or artwork to curate within your home, these mantras will be there with you as reminders that homes are meant to wear in, that it's possible for that to happen beautifully, and that the items within your home are meant to tell your story. While it's almost impossible to adhere to this list of mantras every single time you approach a project, we've found we're happiest with the overall look and feel of a space when we internally repeat them often.

First, we'll consider where your home is located. Every location has its own stories, so our first mantra is to BLUR INDOOR AND OUTDOOR SPACE. Nature truly knows best and offers so much inspiration for the design process. We've found our connection to nature has been enhanced as we bring our favorite pieces outside and our favorite natural elements in.

The next thing to remember is that a home's number one purpose is to be used. It's your protection from the elements, and your place to rest your head, refuel, and love. With that in mind, the next mantra is to CURATE A HOME THAT ENHANCES WITH USE. This is a constant reminder that yes, wood will scratch and fabric will rip, but usually these things happen when we're living in the moment. While wear and tear is impossible to avoid, we can choose materials for our home that celebrate age.

Continuing off of the idea that a home is meant to be used, it's important to consider the actual functionality we desire from our homes as we design them. A home is merely an enclosed space without the experiences held within, therefore our next mantra is to DESIGN FOR ORDINARY EXPERIENCES. As we experience rituals and routines at home, our senses enhance every moment, resulting in sentimental memories. Everyday experiences such as conversation, reading, or eating shape our days, and eventually our years.

With every home, our final mantra is to ALWAYS ADD PLANTS (REAL ONES). They're there to improve air quality, reduce noise, and give us something to nurture. Having something to care for creates more meaning in our lives and increases productivity in other areas. Plants make a home come alive, so we'll also be sharing some of our favorites for both inside and outside our home in the desert.

DESIGN MANTRA #1:
Blur Indoor and Outdoor Space

❖❖❖

A house becomes a home in the context of its surrounding landscape. Our exterior location and culture create home just as much as daily interior space does. While we both grew up in Connecticut and have lived in many other locations since (Baltimore, New York, and San Francisco), Joshua Tree is now the place we call home. With each move, the physical place we've lived in has seeped into the interior design of our space to assist in telling our personal story.

Just outside of a home's windows there are so many visual cues to observe. During the time that we called New York home, we were inspired by hand-painted signs, old penny tiles, and rich charcoal and brick buildings. While living in San Francisco, it was the pastel hues, the abstract quality of the ocean, and the wild succulents that caught our attention. Those influences have come along with us through the years and have built upon each other to develop our personal aesthetic over time.

Looking out the windows at our home in Joshua Tree, we see dusty peaches and greens, patterns of spines on cacti, and textured lizards scurrying before us. The influences of our previous homes have stayed with us, and our new home has now become an accumulation of all of those places. Although, now more than any other location, the influences that find their way into our home are rooted in the nature that surrounds us. Our connection to the sun, the wildlife, and the plants here bring a sense of peace—a feeling we've done our best to incorporate indoors. With large windows looking out to the open desert horizon, and doors leading us directly outside from every room, we've found indoor and outdoor space to blend more than ever before.

Bringing the Indoors Out

Not only have we brought in cues from our landscape—our home is filled with cacti, dusty hues, and sand-colored floors—we've also found ourselves spending considerably more time outside. With some of our closest friends in Joshua Tree, our ritual has become bringing objects typically intended for indoor use outside with us for a few hours. We've enjoyed outdoor movie nights, picnics, and campfires in these temporary and cozy "outdoor living rooms."

Throughout the year, our outdoor gatherings evolve, but the objects used to create these cozy spaces generally remain the same. We've found it doesn't take much more than a side table, a collection of pillows, a bowl or serving board, blankets, and a rug to create a temporary outdoor living room.

OUTDOOR MOVIE NIGHT

Looking up and seeing the stars or the moon for a brief moment, and turning back to an outdoor movie screen surrounded by friends, is one of the best feelings. Warm summer nights when the air is best described as bathwater make this our favorite season for these sorts of gatherings.

Set up your own outdoor movie night by hanging a white sheet in front of your rug, pillows, and blankets. If you have a tall car near your setup, you can use clothespins to secure the sheet to the side of the vehicle. Alternatively, you can purchase an outdoor movie screen or build your own freestanding wooden frame, which you can paint white to create your own space for projections.

Fill up a few bowls of popcorn, curl up in a blanket for the evening, and project your favorite movie (we suggest a classic Western film such as *A Fistfull of Dollars*).

NUTRITIONAL YEAST POPCORN

. . . .

Method

HEAT Using a large 6- to 8-quart stockpot, heat up the coconut oil on medium-high heat. If you find yourself outdoors, try this over a campfire that's been burning for a half hour or so.

POP Add the popcorn seeds and cover. Once the popcorn seeds begin to pop, start shaking the pot back and forth. As soon as the popping stops, turn the stove off and remove the lid. Stir to make sure that the popcorn at the bottom of the pot isn't burning.

SEASON Drizzle half of the olive oil over the popcorn and then stir. Add the rest, and stir again. Repeat this method with the sea salt and nutritional yeast.

ENJOY This popcorn is best enjoyed out under the stars. Fill a large wooden bowl or grouping of small bowls with popcorn for a group of friends.

You'll Need

2 tablespoon coconut oil or alternative high-heat oil

⅓ cup organic popcorn seeds

2 tablespoon olive oil (*We love Wonder Valley olive oil, made by locals to Joshua Tree.*)

1 teaspoon ground coarse sea salt

1½ tablespoon nutritional yeast

GARDEN PICNIC

Our favorite spot at home in Joshua Tree is out in our garden, surrounded by cacti. We love to host small gatherings here, particularly in the late afternoon through sunset with a glass of wine in hand. We've found sunset to be the best reminder to go outside and enjoy the present moment.

To make the evening even sweeter, we love bringing out a collection of vintage board games to play with some fresh chips and salsa.

Our favorite indoor wooden side table, Moroccan poufs, and a Tuareg mat transform our garden into an outdoor living room.

TOMATILLO SALSA RECIPE

Method

CHAR Heat a cast-iron skillet to medium-high. Place the guajillo chiles on the skillet for about one minute on each side, until they puff up and char slightly. Remove the chiles. On the same hot skillet, add the unpeeled garlic cloves, optional jalapeño and habanero for additional spice, and peeled tomatillos for about 6 minutes or until they are softened and slightly charred.

BOIL Discard the stems from the chiles, add the chiles to a medium pot of boiling water, and boil for about 5 minutes or until softened.

BLEND In a food processor or powerful blender, blend the roasted tomatillos, roasted garlic (now peeled), roasted peppers (optional), and drained guajillo chiles with the cumin and salt. Blend the ingredients at medium speed for a textured salsa.

SERVE Serve your homemade salsa with a large wooden bowl full of fresh tortilla chips.

You'll Need

10 dried guajillo chiles

4 garlic cloves

1 jalapeño (optional)

1 habanero (optional)

12 fresh tomatillos

1 tablespoon cumin

2 teaspoon salt

CAMPFIRE GATHERING

There's something particularly special about intimate gatherings around a circle. Maybe it goes back to our roots and the
simple pleasure of sitting around a fire. We've always found this
intimate setting to conjure up conversations of life on other planets, dreams of all sorts, and of course the sounds of an acoustic
guitar. Raw and meaningful moments happen right here next to
the fire and under the stars.

With both a chair and a blanket
for everyone, we gathered
around the campfire to warm our
bodies on a cold desert night.

CLASSIC MEZCAL

Before the fire warms up, serve up a simple shot of mezcal to warm your bones.

Method

Twist the top of each shot glass on a sliced orange to transfer some juice to the rim. Quickly dip the juiced rim into a small bowl of sal de gusano to coat the rim. Serve with a slice of orange.

You'll Need

1 shot of mezcal
(*per person*)

A small bowl of sal de gusano (*the traditional salt for mezcal*)

1 orange, sliced

Bringing the Outdoors In

Designing interior spaces that reflect nature's cycles puts us at ease. If we pay close attention, there are so many natural cues to observe outside, many of them associated with sunlight. Shifting light gives our bodies a natural cycle to follow and gently guides us through the day.

LIGHT

How does your space evolve from day to night? Our home's most natural connection to the sun is through windows, though artificial light indoors has a great impact on this connection and transition through the day as well.

To balance your space, make sure that all lightbulbs throughout your home are of similar warmth. When purchasing bulbs, you'll see on the packaging what color they are classified as. Keeping a consistent warmth throughout your home mimics nature, and using dimmers keeps us in tune with our internal clocks.

Lightbulb Colors

Look for these terms on lightbulb packaging.

WARM WHITE This bulb has a glow that's cozy, calm, and inviting. We use these bulbs in kitchens, living rooms, and bathrooms. Warm white bulbs are also good for commercial spaces and outdoor lighting.

SOFT WHITE This bulb has a warm glow and is brighter than warm white bulbs. We use these bulbs for bedrooms and living spaces.

COOL WHITE This bulb is bright and vibrant. These are good in garages, work areas, and sometimes bathrooms.

DAYLIGHT This bulb is both cool and bright, and it's also one we generally steer clear of when designing homes. Though it's called *daylight*, a bulb this bright does not offer a natural glow.

BRIGHT WHITE This is a bright and cool light with more blue to it, and we generally steer away from this bulb for use in homes.

Dimmers

Dimmers are a wonderful tool to mimic the setting sun, and lower the brightness of light throughout your home when you're ready to settle down for the day. There's no better cue to relax than low lighting.

When installing dimmers, remember that some lightbulbs are not compatible, and that dimmers themselves come in a variety of options made for certain types of bulbs. For example, a dimmer for an incandescent lightbulb may not work with an LED bulb.

COLOR

By designing our home in a generally neutral palette, we have the opportunity to introduce additional colors seasonally. Just as your exterior environment shifts in coloring with the seasons, interior space should evolve as well. In Joshua Tree, many spring blooms, such as those on cacti, desert senna, and creosote bushes, are canary yellow. During this season, we take nature's cue to bring more of this beautiful yellow into our home either with the flowers themselves or by incorporating seasonal textiles with this coloring.

Each season, pay attention to and reconsider your exterior environment's color palette. While in the spring a creosote branch is covered in yellow blooms, summer brings small white poms, and by fall the colors of this plant have faded to rusty greens. By bringing clippings of this native plant indoors, each season's color palette is introduced inside our home.

When the desert landscape is covered in yellow spring blooms, we naturally incorporate more yellows into our home.

Scent

Think about all of the places you've lived and the tiny details you observed along the way. Certainly some of those elements have secretly made their way into your home, but paying close attention to these patterns makes designing a home easier to dissect.

Designing with scent may sound strange, but smell is such a strong component of how we experience home. It's also an incredibly strong trigger for memory, so be conscious of including scents that remind you of your home's exterior environment. For us, this means rosemary and mint shampoo, a fresh branch of creosote in the shower, and sage room spray.

DESIGN MANTRA #2:
Curate a Home
that Enhances with Use

❖ ❖ ❖

A home is not meant to be perfect. It will rarely be perfectly styled, perfectly clean, or perfectly new. Cutting boards will be scraped, mugs will chip, and fabrics will stain. A goal of constant perfection is a setup for disappointment, so when we design a space, we consider the reverse. What if we design our home so that the more it's used, the more beautiful it becomes? What if we could celebrate age as character?

A house becomes a home with the addition of life. This is why it's so important to design a home that's not afraid to be lived in. Not all items will get better with use, but we've found most natural materials enhance with age. Raw brass switch plates oxidize where our fingers search for the light, natural fibers soften, and ceramic glazes crackle over time. These natural characteristics tell the story of an object and remind us that the items we surround ourselves with guide our everyday experiences.

As you bring new or vintage items into your home, it's important to keep the materials with which they're made in mind. We've put together a short guide to our favorite materials, how they age, and examples of how we've used some of them throughout homes we've designed.

Natural Materials Guide

PLASTER

The material of interior walls has the ability to influence the whole look and feel of a space. We personally love the imperfections that plaster shows and the stories that it carries over time. Historically, plaster was made out of lime and sand which would be troweled on over wood lath in old homes. Once drywall became readily available in the 1950s, this method became less popular.

In our home, we used a combination of the two to get the look of plaster with the modern convenience of drywall. Though our walls are made of drywall, we troweled a few coats of a paint plaster combination on top. This technique adds so much warmth and depth to our walls that our home feels like a true hacienda. Below are some plaster types and brands that we've enjoyed using.

American Clay

This is a natural earth plaster made in New Mexico that adds a beautiful texture to any interior, while also being sustainable and environmentally conscious.

Tadelakt

This is a Moroccan technique of making lime plaster waterproof. It is best for plaster applications in a shower, sink, or other areas that might get wet. The plaster is applied in the same method as other plasters, but with the addition of a soap/wax finish for waterproofing. We used this technique for the walls and sink in our bathroom at the Hacienda, with Tadelakt purchased from Atova.

Behr Venetian Plaster

This is an affordable and readily available faux plaster that does a great job of replicating the real thing. Although it comes in a gallon paint can, it is a paint/plaster hybrid that is still applied with a trowel for a depth effect. We used this for our main walls in the Hacienda.

WOOD

There are so many beautiful woods available for home design, but specific varieties have qualities that align well with particular projects. To decide which wood is best for your project, begin by considering your specific needs: Do you need the wood to be hard or soft? Will it be subject to moist conditions? What colors or tones are you drawn to, and what's available in your part of the country?

Also remember that wood does need care and routine conditioning, especially in dry locations like Joshua Tree. Below are some of our favorite types of wood and some examples of when to use them.

Hardwood

Hardwood comes from deciduous trees, which often grow much slower than their pine cousins. Hardwoods are great for furniture since they don't knick or scratch easily. Below are a few of our favorites.

WALNUT Also known as American black walnut or American walnut, this is one of the most beautiful and versatile types of wood in our opinion. We first fell in love with it through mid-century modern furniture, but have grown to appreciate it in implementations that celebrate its raw form and character. It's great for furniture—wood artist Katie Gong made our beautiful live-edge coffee table using this wood.

OAK There are two main groups of oak: white and red. White oak is more resistant to rotting and can be used in outdoor locations, while red oak is best used indoors.

Oak is a wood that we only just recently started to appreciate after seeing local Joshua Tree furniture shop Fire on the Mesa celebrate the imperfections of the wood. For the kitchen cabinets in our Hacienda, Fire on the Mesa used quarter-sawn white oak.

BIRCH AND MAPLE Both of these woods are extremely hard types and can be interchangeable with their light appearance. Birch and maple are often used for cabinets as well as butcher blocks. Birch is also regularly used for plywood.

Softwood

Softwood comes from evergreen conifers and often grows faster than hardwood (this is also why it's cheaper). Softwoods are best used for construction projects. Since these woods scratch easily, they're generally not ideal for furniture.

PINE This is a versatile wood that is both affordable and lightweight. It's used for framing, flooring, and is also great for staining. We used tongue-and-groove pine for our wood ceilings in our home.

DOUGLAS FIR Also used for framing and construction, fir is less prone to warping than pine due to its tighter wood grain. Another benefit to Douglas fir is that it keeps its shape in varying weather, while pine will swell. Most of the standard two-by-fours and plywood available for construction are made of fir.

REDWOOD This is used as a premium building wood. It naturally produces a chemical that makes it insect- and rotproof, so it is great for posts or building materials. Wood artists such as Katie Gong and Aleksandra Zee prefer it for their work as well, with its beautiful warm tone. While it's soft and will show scratches, it ages beautifully. After many uses, redwood will start to tell the story of papers that have been written and nicks that have been formed on its surface.

Veneer

Veneer means a thin strip of wood that you can put over a siding of plywood or other particleboards. Some tables and furniture are completely made of particleboard, covered in veneer to appear as solid wood, which is a way to save on cost without sacrificing a warm and welcoming appearance.

Types of Cuts

The angle at which your wood is cut makes a big difference in the appearance of your project. Generally, plain sawn will work well for almost anything, but if you want to pull out more of the characteristics of wood, quarter sawn is a great option. Lumber is usually cut in one of three ways:

PLAIN SAWN This is the most common cut of wood and yields the least waste with the widest planks. It is what you would typically find in your local hardware store. Growth rings intersect the face of the board at a thirty-degree angle or less.

QUARTER SAWN This is one of the more expensive cuts of wood, partly because it produces additional waste. Its grain is straighter, and sometimes shows beautiful flecking as seen on the white oak cabinetry in the Hacienda's kitchen. In order to be classified as quarter sawn, the growth rings must intersect the face of the board at a sixty- to ninety-degree angle.

RIFT SAWN This cut is also referred to as "radial grain," and can be made from wood left over from quarter sawn. This is the least common and most expensive cut of wood since it also produces the most waste if leftover quarter sawn pieces are not used. Its growth rings usually intersect the face of the board at about forty-five degrees, but can be anywhere between thirty and sixty degrees.

Stain and Wood Finishes

Stains and finishes have the ability to enhance and protect your chosen wood.

BOILED LINSEED OIL This is one of our favorite finishes and what Anthony of Fire on the Mesa used on the oak in our kitchen. It comes in a variety of shades and enhances the grain and character of the wood. Use a beeswax on top of the linseed oil to protect and condition the wood. When applying wax to a surface that will be in contact with food, make sure to get a food-safe wax. Linseed oil requires some maintenance, with yearly reapplications. You'll also need to reapply the beeswax finish to keep the wood conditioned, which is particularly important to us in our dry desert climate.

WOOD STAIN Wood stains are either oil or water based and allow the color of wood to be altered while still letting the grain show through. Some stains will come with a polyurethane finish built in, while others will require an additional varnish, lacquer, polyurethane, or beeswax finish for full protection.

VINEGAR STAIN While we were renovating our home, we noticed some of our wooden window frames needed to be replaced. Though we were using fresh wood, we wanted the window frames to look aged to match the aesthetic of the rest of our home. To achieve the aged appearance, we created a vinegar stain.

To create your own vinegar stain, add a piece of steel wool to a gallon of white vinegar and allow it to sit for a week. Once the vinegar has turned brown, wipe it onto new wood with a rag and watch the grain darken. Be careful not to apply too much stain, since as it dries it will darken considerably. Once the vinegar is dry, sand the wood so that the vinegar stain only shows on the wood grain, giving the wood an aged appearance. Wood stain or linseed oil can then be applied over top of the vinegar stain.

WAX Wax is a clear finish used to protect wood. Apply wax after staining for a water-resistant finish. Wax will need to be reapplied regularly to keep the wood protected.

VARNISH This is a hard and durable finish that can be applied either to raw wood or over a stain. If applying to wood that's outdoors, spar varnish will protect it from ultraviolet light as well as water.

LACQUER This is an extremely hard, durable, and clear finish that can be applied over paint or stain. Most lacquer finishes are sprayed on, but there are also varieties available that can be brushed on.

SHELLAC This natural material, harvested from resin secreted from the female lac bug comes in a clear or amber color. Once the resin is combined with ethanol, it creates shellac. This finish is great on furniture, but shouldn't come into contact with heat, which will leave a white ring.

POLYURETHANE This comes in oil- or water-based options and is a type of liquid plastic that dries clear. It comes in any sheen that you want and is easily brushed on or applied with a rag. We often use the water-based poly since it's less toxic and works great for our projects.

However, if your wood will come in contact with heat, it's best to use an oil-based poly since the water-based version will leave rings. Oil-based poly is also thicker than its water-based counterpart—one coat of oil-based poly is the equivalent of a few coats of water-based poly. If you are using an oil-based poly, scrub with a piece of fine steel wool between coats. For water-based poly, use 400 or 500 grit sandpaper since the steel wool will leave a rust residue. When sanding, make sure to sand in the direction of the wood grain.

PAINT AND PRIMER

Paint has an incredible ability to quickly alter a space's mood and lighting, and is key to many interior projects.

Primer

Before applying a coat of paint, a coat of primer is the first step. It's helpful both for bonding paint to a surface and for covering over other colors. When beginning a project, make sure to get the correct type of primer depending on your surface material. For example, if you're painting on metal, a primer is available specifically for that. There are also primers made for covering over wood knots or stains.

Paint

Paint comes in different qualities and sheens. In our opinion it's worth splurging on the best-quality paint in your price range for an appearance that will stand the test of time. Paint usually comes in matte/flat, eggshell, satin, semigloss, and gloss. For interior walls we use matte or eggshell, but for kitchens and bathrooms satin or semigloss is best to repel moisture and grease. When choosing your sheen, keep in mind that higher sheens will highlight more surface imperfections.

Paint and Primer

This combination has become a popular option at paint stores and can work well for many projects. That said, you get what you pay for. While it's more convenient to have paint and primer all rolled into one, nothing compares to the quality of rolling on primer and paint separately.

PLANTERS

Planters are made from a variety of materials including clay, terra-cotta, fiberglass, and metal. We love planters made from natural materials, and many of the planters we have chosen consist of clay and brass. Any kind of vessel can be used as a planter, but always make sure that your pot has a drainage hole to prevent root rot.

Clay and Ceramic

Planters made with these materials usually come glazed and are best for indoor use. Our favorite ceramic planters are made by independent artists such as Joshua Tree local Brian Bosworth of BKB Ceramics, but we also enjoy classic ones by Gainey and Heath Ceramics. Over time, we've collected many vintage clay and ceramic planters from flea markets and swap meets as well.

TERRA-COTTA These pots are unglazed clay with iron deposits that give the surface a beautiful red tint. These planters are also generally made in a heavier style, with thicker walls, which make a suitable environment for most plants. Terra-cotta has a long history, with pottery made from the material still around from hundreds of years ago.

Brass

We love brass, particularly as it tarnishes and ages, and are always on the lookout for brass vessels that can be used as indoor planters.

TILE

There are so many incredible materials used to make tile, such as natural stone, ceramic, and glass.

Terra-cotta

This is a tile made from red and brown clay. It has lovely earth tones with iron deposits that create irregular coloring. The use of this tile adds a warmth found in many hacienda-style homes. We have used it for floor tiles and roof tiles at the Hacienda and the Joshua Tree House. Make sure to add a sealant to terra-cotta floor tiles after installation so that they repel water and stains.

Recycled Tile

Fireclay Tile based out of San Francisco is one of our favorite tile sources, especially for their use of recycled tile. Their designs come in a variety of shapes, sizes, and colors. They offer beautiful hand-painted tiles as well.

Moroccan

These tiles are handmade with clay using techniques from the Mediterranean region. They're often slightly irregular shapes and thicknesses, which imparts the essence of a handmade home to any space. We used Zellige tiles in the bathroom of the Hacienda and love the irregular look they add to our shower.

Talavera

This is a Mexican hand-painted tile with designs that vary from piece to piece. These are great for an accent tile and can often be found along stair risers or used as backsplashes.

Natural Stone

Our favorite stone for floors is flagstone for its raw and organic shape. Natural stone is also quite porous, so make sure to add a sealant after installation to confirm that it's waterproof.

METAL

When deciding on types of metals to use for your home's fixtures, switch plates, and trim details, try to pick one and stick to it throughout your home. It's a small detail that will make your design feel cohesive.

Brass

This is an absolute favorite of ours right now. We particularly love using raw brass and watching it age over time. When buying a brass fixture, pay attention to whether it's raw or polished. We personally prefer a raw or brushed finish over polished for a relaxed aesthetic. Over time brass will oxidize to tell stories of the people who interacted with it. If you want the raw brass look but don't want it to visibly age, you may want to go with a brushed metal finish or regularly clean your brass with soap and water.

Stainless Steel

This metal has been a classic in homes for quite a while now. It doesn't rust, which works well for bathroom and kitchen sink fixtures as well as silverware.

Raw Steel

Often used for furniture legs, this is a beautiful metal with natural blemishes and an industrial look.

Wrought Iron

Used for industrial lighting and accessories, this is an iron that's been hammered into shape. Expect to find more blemishes and inconsistencies on its surface.

Copper

This warm metal can be found in different types of lighting, cookware, and kitchen fixtures and sinks. It has a beautiful reddish-brown color and will oxidize to a green over time without consistent care.

STAINED GLASS

This material is beautiful in both small and large applications. It has the ability to turn windows into murals, and in smaller applications can still allow beautiful colored light to stream into your home. Stained glass artists Kathrin Smirke of Bands of Color and Steve Halterman of The Station are both local to Joshua Tree.

Stained glass artwork by
Kathrin Smirke

FABRIC

Every time you walk across a room, sit on a chair, or lay in your bed, you're interacting with fabric. This material adds so much warmth to a home and offers sound absorbency as well. Natural fabrics create homes that are not afraid to be lived in.

Wool

This is a warm fiber taken from sheep. When buying wool, always look for used or vintage wool first, since not all wool producers have humane practices. We love searching for used wool blankets, kilim or Moroccan rugs, and pillows at vintage and thrift shops. Alpaca and mohair are other options similar to wool.

Linen

Loose and airy, this is an absolutely beautiful fabric. Made from flax, it's also considered to be one of the world's strongest natural fibers. Linen works wonderfully on duvets, pillows, napkins, towels, curtains, and blankets. It's also one of our favorite fabrics for clothing throughout the summer here in Joshua Tree.

Leather

This natural material, taken from the hide of various animals, wears in beautifully and ages well over time. When buying leather, look for dead stock or surplus leather that was otherwise going to be disposed of. If that isn't an option, try to find ethical leather that was sourced locally, which helps to cut down on carbon emissions.

Canvas

This is an extremely strong and durable fabric made of linen or cotton that reminds us of vintage tents and workwear. It's also fairly water-resistant, so it's a great fabric to use in areas with a lot

of wear and tear. You'll often find canvas used on safari chairs, heavyweight curtains, and duffel bags.

Sunbrella

This fabric is great for outdoor use and the only one that we've found to hold up to the intense sunlight and heat of the desert.

Cotton

A classic found in many applications, this material is made from the cotton plant and can be incredibly soft depending on the thread count. It's the perfect material for bedding, blankets, towels, and clothing.

Storied Rugs

Scattered throughout our home are rugs of varying natural materials. We deliberately choose rugs with colors, textures, and patterns that allow us to live freely. If a drink spills, it's no big deal. Natural materials clean well, and truly get better with age.

Moroccan rugs in particular have stolen our hearts as a dependable way to inject soul into a home. Created by Moroccan Berbers who live amid nature, these rugs are both inspired by and created with materials from their surrounding landscape.

We've learned an incredible amount about these rugs from Taib Lotfi and Kenya Knight, owners of Palm Springs Moroccan rug shop Soukie Modern. Taib grew up in the Adgar village of Morocco, is a self-proclaimed "rug addict," and has shared with us the many stories behind each tribe's signature styles. Moroccan rugs are art, a celebration of marriage, and a way to impress special guests—they are seating, they are bedding, they are income. Seamlessly woven into the fabric of Moroccan lives, they tell many stories.

SOUKIE MODERN'S MOROCCAN RUG GUIDE

Originally Moroccan rugs were made from 100 percent Berber sheep wool, and in some tribes goat hair. Over time cotton yarn was utilized as a convenient and affordable addition to this roster of materials. One of the most ingenious adaptations in this process was when weavers realized they could upcycle used articles of clothing and turn them into rugs called *boucherouite* (an Arabic term meaning a piece of torn clothing). These rugs are also referred to as "rag rugs" by Western cultures.

Taib tells from his experience that when you walk into a home with boucherouite rugs it can be an indication that the family does not have many sheep and therefore may not be as wealthy. The fact that Berber weavers endeavored to create carpets despite a lack of wool resulted in some of the most decorative, jubilant, and triumphant works.

Ait Bou Ichaouen (aka Talsint)

HIGH ATLAS MOUNTAINS

The Ait Bou Ichaouen tribe hails from the High Atlas Mountains. Traditionally Berbers put tribes first, but over time most tribes accepted Moroccan rule and Islam. The tribe most resistant to conformity was the Ait Bou Ichaouen—so much so that they retreated to an incredibly remote area to be left to their own people and their own ways. They fought off the French, who were in pursuit of their land for twenty-six years, and they sparred with neighboring tribes. They have fierce warrior hearts and a love and dedication to their family. To this day most Ait Bou Ichaouen live a nomadic lifestyle in tents, affording the tribe an abundance of sheep that can be herded to graze in optimal locations depending on the time of year. Their masses of sheep provided them with wealth and also some of the most spectacular silky wool available.

From here, the story gets even more incredible. Ait Bou Ichaouen rugs were undiscovered by outsiders until 1997. The tribe lived so remotely and in such a difficult area to access (the way they liked it!) that their rugs were unknown to the carpet market until some adventurous dealers decided to take the broken and challenging road less traveled to see what they could find. These adventurers were rewarded with a treasure trove of never-before-seen rugs. The fact that this was their first meeting with dealers meant the tribe had no news or guidance from the market influencing them on how to make their rugs. Their rugs were purely created in alignment with their aesthetic values and incredible connection to the earth. These mountain people yield some of the most passionate and stunning rugs using bold colors and symbolic motifs. Their isolation allowed for a time capsule effect in their craftsmanship, which offers an almost lost, truly authentic, old-world North African–style symbolism and weaving technique.

Azilal
HIGH ATLAS MOUNTAINS

Azilal rugs are known for their abstract and avant-garde style of weaving. They're single knotted, which allows for very fine work and artistic designs. Often made from silky undyed sheep's wool with a neutral ivory base, these rugs utilize brown or black wool to create diamond and lattice designs with henna-dyed golden accents.

Beni M'Guild
MIDDLE ATLAS MOUNTAINS

Beni M'Guild rugs tend to be very plush, woven to provide warmth and comfort during the winter months. Typically woven to be reversible with an equally stunning flat surface, the pile side faces downward for warmer months.

Beni Ourain
MIDDLE ATLAS MOUNTAINS

The Beni Ourain tribe resides in the Middle Atlas region of Morocco. Beni Ourain carpets possess a neutral geometric look which blends beautifully with the clean lines of modern furniture and architecture. These rugs primarily have a creamy off-white background, and black or brown wool is used to add free-form geometric lines and diamonds.

The sheep of the Beni Ourain tribe are an ancient breed that yields stunning silky long wool. Labeled "the huge whites" by Henri Matisse, these rugs have inspired many European artists such as Alvar Aalto, Le Corbusier, and Paul Klee. While copying

may be the highest form of flattery, the Beni Ourain style of rug is the most appropriated by mass-market manufacturers, typically yielding machine-made versions with perfectly symmetrical lines. However, we always encourage buyers to appreciate the subtle variations and imperfections in authentic Moroccan rugs. It is said that Berber tribal weavers feel that only God should endeavor to be perfect and therefore deliberate asymmetry is a beautiful and appreciated aspect of each piece.

Boucherouite
ALL TRIBES

Moroccan boucherouite rugs are woven by Berber tribal women for domestic use in the home. The word *boucherouite* stems from the Arabic *bu sherwit* meaning "a scrap from used clothing." Indeed, these whimsical works of art are made from recycled cloth and are both durable and warming to any space. Easy to clean, a boucherouite rug is suitable for spaces experiencing heavy foot traffic. The humble origins of these rugs serve only to accentuate the remarkable nature of the finished products. Upcycling at its highest level, the talented Berber weaver makes art out of scraps.

Boujad
PLAINS

The Boujad region is a widespread area rather than one tribal confederation. While there is the commonality of weaving with the same knotting technique, there are varying styles of Boujad carpets. The knot used is a tight one that requires less wool, resulting in a low pile. This low pile allows for more geometric, intricate, and abstract designs, something Boujad carpets are known for.

Kilim
ALL TRIBES

The word *kilim* is of Turkish origins, and it is likely the Turks of the Ottoman Empire who passed on kilim weaving techniques to the Berber tribes. In Morocco they call kilim rugs "Hanabel." These low-pile flat-weave rugs are made in Turkey, North Africa, the Middle East, central Asia, and China, and their lighter weight makes them perfect for hot summer months. Moroccan kilim rugs can be made with wool, cotton, silk, and even animal hair. Kilims are commonly used on the floors and walls in Berber tents.

Ourika
HIGH ATLAS MOUNTAINS

The Ourika Valley is south of Marrakesh along the northern slopes of the High Atlas. Their cold rivers make it harder to spindle and clean the wool extensively, and therefore Ourika rugs tend to have a chunkier, soft, blanketlike character. These beautiful rugs are worked in undyed cream and brown wool. After the 1990s, Ourika tribal weavers began to add a lot of color in their designs with cotton yarn. These rugs are woven with larger spaces between the knots, making the rug more malleable and comfortable to rest on.

Tuareg
PRINCIPALLY SAHARA DESERT

While not hailing from Morocco, Tuaregs are a large Berber confederation and have cultural aspects in common, so we have included them in this list of Moroccan rugs. Produced primarily in the early twentieth century when nomadic tribes migrated through North Africa, these mats are easily rolled up, making them suitable for tribes on the move. The tents where Tuaregs lived and celebrated were furnished with these mats, used both as floor and wall coverings. Made of dwarf palm fibers and stitched with designs in camel or goat leather, these rugs are very durable and created to withstand the hottest desert temperatures.

Zanafi
HIGH ATLAS MOUNTAINS

The Zanafi flat-weave rug is composed of patterned bands and widely thought of as closest to what original Berber rugs may have been like. Their design was multifunctional—the same banded weaving was also used to make transport bags to carry things like grains and goods.

CARING FOR MOROCCAN RUGS

Moroccan rugs truly stand the test of time. Weavers put incredible care and attention into shaving the wool, spindling it, and tying the most durable knots. Barring any accidental damage, normal use and proper cleaning should allow for a beautiful appearance for decades.

Boucherouite rugs that are small enough to fit in a washing machine can be cleaned at home. We like to use a fragrance-free detergent and dry the rug in the sun Moroccan style. Otherwise, it's always best to clean your rugs with a professional, though we suggest steering clear of chemicals. We've seen many beautiful Moroccan rugs taken to the dry cleaners only to be ruined. The chemicals from that type of cleaning process can alter the color of the dyes and give the wool an odor. To care for your one-of-a-kind work of art properly, take it to a professional versed in this type of cleaning to make sure it's perfectly maintained.

Embracing Accidents with *Kintsugi*

Items in a home are like the chapters of a book—each item telling a portion of a life story. Inevitably over time, our homes will scar just as we do. The beautiful opportunity that comes next is to embrace and even celebrate those scars and the stories that they tell.

The Japanese art form of *kintsugi* ("golden joinery") embraces this mentality fully. Cracks and breaks in pottery are elevated with beautiful repairs. Lacquer is mixed with powdered gold or other metals to accentuate the breakage lines. Rather than mourning over broken pottery, you'll find yourself enjoying the way in which each crack formed as gravity's own artwork.

For us, *kintsugi* is a reminder that everything's okay, and that an object only has as much value as we personally assign it. One winter evening, a tiny mouse made its way into our home in search of warmth, only to find our two cats there to greet her. A typical cat and mouse chase ensued, during which one of our cats bumped into a cabinet sending one of our favorite planters crashing to the ground. A series of subsequent emotions such as shock or sadness could have easily turned this moment into a negative one. But with a slight shift in perspective, accidents like this can remind us of the chaos that life often brings, the loved ones that surround us, and that accidents can be beautiful if we allow them to be.

Broken items can come with a preconceived story of negativity, but in embracing accidents we realized that the repair itself has the ability to enhance the beauty of the object. Rather than feel disappointment over a broken planter, we now prefer to use the event as an excuse to create a new piece of art that tells the story of what happened. The art of *kintsugi* also saves us from the wastefulness of throwing away broken items, while offering an opportunity for acceptance. The way in which we react to each moment is what ultimately determines a good day or a bad one—every moment is what we make it.

PRACTICE THIS AT HOME

In the traditional *kintsugi* method, natural adhesive from lacquer trees (*Toxicodendron vernicifluum*) is used to repair broken pottery. After one to two weeks of drying time, real gold powder is then dusted over a second layer of lacquer which is again left to dry. The total process can take months, but the outcome is stunning.

Inspired by traditional *kintsugi*, we've developed the method below as an approachable alternative to appreciating accidents and imperfections. If you'd like to try the traditional method, there are also many kits available online by searching "kintsugi kit."

REPAIRING CRACKS

Use this method if your pottery has cracked into multiple pieces.

Repair Crack

Apply a very thin coat of glue to the broken edges of the pottery, and hold firmly together until tacky. Wipe any excess glue off with a damp towel, and use masking tape to hold the pottery together until the glue is completely dry (fully cures in about 24–48 hours).

You'll Need

Broken pottery (*You'll need all of the pieces.*)

E6000 or other multipurpose glue

Damp towel

Masking tape

REPAIRING A MISSING PIECE

The below method inspired by *kintsugi* will fill in missing pieces if parts of your pottery have crumbled.

Method

MIX EPOXY PUTTY Combine the epoxy parts until thoroughly mixed.

APPLY Epoxy generally dries within 5 minutes, so immediately apply to your ceramic piece where there is a part missing. Use the epoxy to fill in the gaps, and smooth the epoxy with your fingers as much as possible (while wearing gloves).

DRY Allow the epoxy to dry. (Most epoxies take around 1 hour to fully cure.)

SAND Sand the dried epoxy until it is completely smooth and flush with the original ceramic.

You'll Need

Broken pottery (*Missing pieces are okay.*)

Ceramic epoxy putty

400–500 grit sandpaper

Biodegradable disposable gloves

CELEBRATE THE IMPERFECTIONS

Method

APPLY LIQUID GOLD LEAF Now it's time to honor the beauty of the breakages by painting the repaired cracks with gold. Use your superfine paintbrush to delicately paint over the repair lines and filled in areas. Allow the liquid gold leaf to fully cure before putting your pottery back to use.

This *kintsugi*-inspired method is generally best for repairing ceramics that do not come in contact with food, as most liquid gold leaf is not food-safe.

You'll Need

Liquid gold leaf

Superfine paintbrush

Turpenoid natural brush cleaner

Paper towel

DESIGN MANTRA #3:
Design for Ordinary Experiences

◆ ◆ ◆

Ordinary is our everyday, it's our routine. With a focus on the present moment, ordinary pulls us into what's happening now. Ultimately, the ordinary makes up who we are as people and is everything that a home is built for. Through everyday acts we find a comfort in simplicity and a form of happiness that can't be taken away. If small, ordinary moments shape our lives and we find immense pleasure in them, then we are set free.

By definition ordinary is not special, but we've found that statement to be far from the truth. As the first rural place either of us has lived, our time here in Joshua Tree has brought new meaning to the word. If ordinary is taking a bath, drinking tea from a favorite mug, or watching the sunrise, then heck, we'll take it. Ordinary is our treasure.

When designing your everyday space, it's worth considering how design can gently enhance ordinary experiences. The corners of a home come alive when music is played, coffee is brewed, and conversations are enjoyed. Ordinary experiences are often overlooked as mundane, but ultimately they are what compose our lives.

There's a reason we feel sentimental when remembering watching movies or making tea while a storm brewed outside. At its most basic, home is protection from the elements such as wind or rain—it's a sentimental place that offers the simple comfort of shelter. Other ordinary experiences at home include bathing, sleeping, daydreaming, cooking, eating, drinking, conversation, and reading. All of these everyday occurrences have the potential to be special, with a few considerate touches.

Bathing

Showers and baths are ordinary experiences that we're incredibly grateful to have access to, particularly in the desert. Though it's easy to overlook repetitive moments of the day, these ordinary rituals shape our lives.

Tie a bundle of creosote (also known as chaparral) to your showerhead with a cotton string for an invigorating scent. After a rainstorm, the desert fills with petrichor: the distinctive earthy scent of rainfall on hot dry soil and plants. The smell of wet creosote in particular is a reminder of soaking desert rains and a signifier to be mindful of water consumption in our dry climate. If you don't have access to creosote, try a bundle of eucalyptus instead. The two plants can also be combined for a hardy bundle that can last a month or so in your shower.

CREOSOTE SHOWER BUNDLE

Method

Gather a bundle of creosote (a resinous native plant found abundantly throughout the Mojave Desert) about two inches in diameter. When gathering, keep in mind that it is illegal to take any plant life from national parks. Tie and knot a twelve-inch strand of cotton string around the branches of the plant, and hang this upside down from your showerhead. Turn your shower to warm water, and enjoy the ritual of hydration and bathing with the aroma of desert rain.

You can also thoughtfully select other scents in the shower that trigger sentimental memories. Shampoo, conditioner, and body wash all have the ability to encourage daydreams of your favorite places.

You'll Need

Creosote

Eucalyptus (*optional addition or can be used in replacement of creosote*)

12-inch strand of cotton string

Scissors

SLEEPING

A quality pillow is often overlooked, but has made our bed at home a daily treat to return to. Rather than waiting for a grand getaway or far-off experience, remember that days are the foundation of our years.

Pay attention to your sleeping habits. Do you sleep on your side, stomach, or back? There are pillows available to choose from for each sleeping habit. It's a simple thing, but spending a little time and money on this small detail can turn your bed at home into your own personal sanctuary. To enhance the experience of sleep even more, spray your pillow with a lavender spray or dab with essential oil before laying down for the night.

It's also important to keep the area around your bed clean and clear of distraction for a good night's sleep. Try hanging a simple canopy over your bed to add a bit of romanticism and a sense of calm.

LINEN BED CANOPY

Method

STAIN DOWELS Use a rag to wipe your chosen stain color evenly across the wooden dowels.

MEASURE Find the center of the ceiling above your bed and hold the dowel up to the ceiling parallel with it. Mark the ends of the dowel with a pencil. Measure about 2–3 inches inward on either side to find where you will install your brass hooks. Make sure that the width of your fabric will fit between the brass hooks with extra room to spare. You can always fold the width of your fabric in half if it was from a wide bolt.

INSTALL HOOKS Install your brass hooks in the 2 locations marked. Depending on the hardness of your ceiling, you may need to drill 2 pilot holes before hand-screwing the hooks in place.

REPEAT Repeat this process for the 2 outer dowels, but this time bring your dowels all the way to the walls on either side of your bed.

HANG Once your hooks are in place, fold the length of your fabric in half. Hang the center fold of fabric over your center dowel, and slot the dowel into the center set of brass hooks. You may need to use pliers to adjust the hooks to fit your dowel properly. Repeat this process on the outer dowels.

TRIM Use a pair of scissors to trim the ends of the fabric down if needed. This simple canopy looks beautiful with the ends slightly pooled onto the floor.

You'll Need

3 wooden dowels

Your choice of stain

Rag for stain

6 brass-plated steel cup hooks (These are half hook, half screw.)

A length of linen from your local fabric store (2x wall height + wall width + 2 extra yards to account for drapage)

Scissors

Pencil

DAYDREAMING

Daydreams are the best kind of dreams—night dreams can be fleet-ing, but capturing moments throughout the day to allow your mind to freely wander is a great way to remain playful and realize your goals all at once.

Large windows at home transport us. We keep a box of mark-ers, colored pencils, and notebooks easily accessible and ready to document our daydreams. This practice frees our minds.

COOKING

Cooking is the perfect opportunity to stay fully present. Focus on the meal you're about to create, and let to-do lists and conversations you've been holding on to fade away. Beginning with a clean kitchen, bring deliberate and mindful movements into your cooking process: slow breaths, with a dedicated focus on the preparation of your ingredients.

A quality knife, a good cutting board, and cookware that's both beautiful and functional (we love collecting vintage Dansk cookware) will make the process all the more enjoyable. While you're at it, choose a favorite record to put on while you cook.

EATING

Remember that food is art, and plating it is a part of the experience. Living in the desert means that we don't often go out to eat, so our home has become our own personal restaurant. Collect a couple of dishware options to choose from, depending on the type of food to be plated. Mexican pottery enhances a breakfast of chilaquiles just as Year & Day plates and flatware serve as a simple and modern backdrop for an outdoor celebratory dinner with friends.

Whether shopping at our local health food market, farmers' market, or grocery store, we bring our reusable netted bags with us. Not only are they incredibly functional (they don't take up much space and expand), they're also beautiful. We leave a grouping of them hanging by our front door as a reminder to bring them with us and love that they look great collected there as well.

DRINKING

A collection of curated mugs is a really simple way to make the experience of drinking tea or coffee at home special. When drinking water, add something fresh like lemon or basil to find more joy in staying hydrated. We also love to add large ice cubes to a cocktail, creating the feeling of a cocktail bar at home.

CONVERSATION

Keep a stack of blankets in your living room, enough for you and a group of friends. This simple act of bundling up in a blanket adds an immediate sense of comfort and opens your home to more intimate conversation. Visually, a stack of blankets adds texture and color to your home, while also offering sound absorbency.

When deciding on the layout of your living room, remember that circular furniture arrangements make for great conversation. If space allows, turn two or more chairs or poufs toward your sofa so that when friends come over everyone not only has a place to sit, but can also see and hear each other clearly.

Consider the senses, as with the sound and vibration of a record player.

Create spaces for intimate
conversation at home.

READING

Since moving to the desert, our obsession with collecting vintage books has grown exponentially. We wander off to our local swap meet to collect piles of old plant guides, trail guides, and books full of home inspiration. We've found the simplest pleasure in sitting down with a good book and staying off of our phones for a while.

Reading becomes even more freeing while in a hanging chair or hammock. These playful forms of seating stimulate movement and creativity.

CONSIDER ALL OF THE SENSES

Finally, it's important to consider all of the senses as their own ordinary experiences. A record player loses its meaning without the vibration of sound in the corner of your living room, and a candle loses its allure without the context of a bath. The sensory experience of a home is what leaves us with warm memories, and influences how we feel. How we feel at home greatly contributes to how we feel in general, so it's important to consider how design can guide the ordinary and sensory experiences of each day.

The smallest details sometimes make the most impact, and considered design elements do not need to be grand or expensive. As Charles Eames said, "The details are not the details. They make the design."

A Joseph's coat cactus and an
old man cactus grouped together
contrast each other in color,
texture, and shape.

DESIGN MANTRA #4
Always Add Plants (Real Ones)

◈ ◈ ◈

Even the warmest interiors feel sterile without the addition of plants. Not only do plants draw our nurturing qualities to the surface, they improve air quality and bring a home to life. We're convinced that a home cannot be filled with too many indoor plants—they can be hung from the ceiling in macramé planters or planted in pots of varying colors, shapes, and sizes. Groupings of plants throughout a home create sculptural compositions that consider color, form, and texture.

Mojave Desert Plant Guide

JOSHUA TREE
Yucca brevifolia

Joshua Tree National Park's namesake is claimed to have been Dr. Seuss's inspiration for truffula trees; they are goofy and otherworldly in appearance. The Joshua tree is not actually a tree, but rather a plant due to its fibrous growth patterns and lack of trunk rings. Joshua trees are incredibly slow growers, growing only around one-half inch to three inches per year. Joshua trees are usually one of the first plants to bloom each year, beginning in February. Their blooms grow in clusters at the end of their branches, which appear to be a greenish-white color. Scientists believe that in order for a Joshua tree to bloom, the branch ends must freeze in the winter. After the tree blooms, it's pollinated by a yucca moth which also lays her eggs in the plant ovaries.

CREOSOTE
Larrea tridentata

This common bush in the Mojave has stolen our hearts. It can be easily overlooked as a weed, but its small resinous leaves, striped branches, scent of desert rains, and yellow blooms from April to May have made this plant most sentimental to us. It conquers the desert, growing abundantly in an unforgiving environment. It can live thousands of years—the oldest creosote found is called King Clone and estimated to be about 11,700 years old, making it one of the oldest living organisms on our planet! You can visit King Clone in the Creosote Rings Preserve in Lucerne Valley, California.

TEDDY BEAR CHOLLA
Cylindropuntia bigelovii

While this type of cholla cactus appears soft and cuddly, it's incredibly sharp and dangerous. There are small hooks at the ends of the spines that grab onto skin, making them difficult to remove. The joints of this cholla easily detach and hitch rides with hikers or other animals to spread the plant's seed. These cacti are found all over the Mojave, but one of the most beautiful clusters can be found at the Cholla Cactus Garden in Joshua Tree National Park. If you happen to visit between March and May, you may witness them bloom one of the few naturally green flowers.

PENCIL CHOLLA
Cylindropuntia ramosissima

This is another type of cholla cactus with narrow stems resembling a pencil. These cacti put out a pinkish-orange flower later in the season (around May to June).

DESERT SENNA
Senna armata

This bush displays yellow blooms from April to May and is most commonly found in sand washes. Most of the year, it appears as pastel green and blue branches. On the rare occasion that the desert experiences fog, these plants make us feel as though we're walking along the ocean floor. Its beautiful colors and shape have made senna a favorite for arranging in a vase or as a table setting.

CALIFORNIA JUNIPER
Juniperus californica

Found throughout the higher elevations of Joshua Tree, this tree historically offered shade, medicine, and food to Native Americans. It can grow up to thirty feet tall and puts out berries annually, which can be used to cook with. You can find juniper trees on the Pine City Trail, Jumbo Rocks Campground, Keys View, Geology Tour Road, and many other locations in Joshua Tree National Park.

BEAVERTAIL CACTUS
Opuntia basilaris

This plant grows in mounds of paddles and always seems to be the first cactus to bloom each spring with vibrant fuchsia flowers. Just after moving to Joshua Tree full-time, we saw a bright pink cluster out in the distance. We walked out to it, and discovered a giant and breathtaking beavertail cactus in full bloom. The paddles of a beavertail may look like they don't have spines, but they actually have bristles that are both difficult to remove and painful. Removing these bristles from clothing can be nearly impossible, as they are difficult to see.

MANZANITA
Arctostaphylos glauca

This plant looks like shrubs or small trees that are easily recognizable by their red tree trunks, signifying a healthy plant. They have small, waxy leaves and produce little berries in spring and summer. Manzanitas grow all through the park, but you can specifically find them in Barker Dam or Pioneertown Mountains Preserve.

Hedgehog cactus

California juniper

PIÑON PINE
Pinus monophylla

This tree is often found at altitudes above 3,000 feet, which is perfect for Joshua Tree National Park. They grow tasty piñon nuts which were a traditional Native American food source. Look for these beautiful pines on the Pine City Trail.

HEDGEHOG CACTUS
Echinocereus coccineus

This is an erect cylindrical cactus that grows in clusters. It puts out a vibrant red or pink flower in the spring and can be found throughout Joshua Tree National Park.

MULLER OAK
Quercus cornelius-mulleri

This is a tree or shrub that we often see confidently growing in the creases of boulders. It has dense branches with thick and shiny green leaves and can be found throughout the park, but we've seen many beautiful examples at Barker Dam specifically.

CALIFORNIA BARREL CACTUS
Ferocactus cylindraceus

This is a red spherical cactus that grows curved spines as it ages. They can be found along mountainsides in the park or right off trails in washes. Keep an eye out for these cacti on your next hike through Joshua Tree—you'll often find them growing straight out of the boulders.

MORMON TEA
Ephedra nevadensis

This green shrub with dense jointed twigs and branches is often found in washes. Native Americans and Mormons used these branches for medicinal tea and drinks once they would dry out. In the spring they have small yellow blooms.

MOJAVE YUCCA
Yucca schidigera

This is a cousin to the Joshua Tree and often confused with them. Usually found on rocky slopes, the yucca can grow up to sixteen feet tall, though they are often found in shorter clusters. The main telltale difference between a Joshua tree and yucca besides height is the long curly fibers that grow from the yucca's pointy leaves. The yucca's flowers and fruits are similar to those of the Joshua tree and bloom around the same time as well. Native Americans used the leaves to make sandals and clothing, while the roots were used for soap. Yuccas can be found all throughout Joshua Tree National Park.

Desert fan palm

CHEESEBUSH
Ambrosia salsola

Aptly named, this plant can have the smell of cheese and is found in washes where it has access to occasional water. In March through June it puts out small white flowers that fall as the heat intensifies through the summer. Cheesebushes can be found on Barker Dam Trail.

DESERT FAN PALM
Washingtonia filifera

These palms are often found near streams, oases, or other water sources in the desert. They can grow to around sixty feet tall and can be seen at the Fortynine Palms Oasis, the Oasis of Mara, Lost Palms Oasis, and Indian Canyon in Palm Springs. A hike under these wise trees is magical and serves as a perfect spot for an afternoon picnic.

MOJAVE PRICKLY PEAR
Opuntia polyacantha

This is a type of cactus with paddles, which usually grows up to two feet tall. They bloom in yellowish flowers that fade to oranges and pinks in the late spring. Prickly pears also grow fruit called a tuna, which is an invaluable food source to native animals such as the desert tortoise. The tuna can be eaten or juiced once the spines and seeds are removed.

PAPERBAG BUSH
Salazaria mexicana

This is a shrub that can grow to be a few feet tall. It has small "paper bag" flowers at the end of the branches that start off with a purple tint, but eventually turn beige as they die. These are often found in washes and rocky slopes.

CALIFORNIA BUCKWHEAT
Eriogonum fasciculatum

This plant has dense branches and can be found in washes in the open desert. In the spring, it puts out white flowers that turn into a rusty red as they dry out. Native Americans used buckwheat for medicinal purposes, and today the plant can also be employed as flour for things like buckwheat pancakes or noodles.

Outdoor Plant Guide

PURPLE PRICKLY PEAR
Opuntia macrocentra

This cactus is native to the southwestern United States and northern Mexico. It's easily a favorite plant of ours due to its purple coloring and contrast with the desert environment. It grows from one to three feet and bears beautiful yellow flowers in the spring.

FAT BOY CACTUS
Helianthocereus terscheckii

This cactus resembles a saguaro, but grows much faster. It can grow up to a foot a year, reaching ten to twenty feet tall. After many years it will produce arms as well. In the spring and fall, they will grow an arm, which begins as what looks like a small cotton ball and subsequently puts out a large white flower. It usually blooms overnight and will close up by midday, so be sure to rise early when the fat boy cactus is about to bloom.

PALO VERDE
Parkinsonia florida

These trees are typically found in the Southwest and the Sonoran Desert. They have green trunks with spines, put out yellow flowers in the spring, and can grow to around twenty feet tall.

Fat boy cactus

Cow tongue cactus

MESQUITE
Prosopis glandulosa

These trees can reach a height of twenty to thirty feet and offer good shade in the desert. They are very tough trees with thorns that can grow up to several inches long! It's important to keep the area under a mesquite tree well maintained so you don't step on a thorn (we're speaking from experience).

GOLDEN SPINED CEREUS
Bergerocactus emoryi

These are thin cacti that are often found in groups. Sometimes they stick up toward the sky, and other times they appear to be slithering along the ground just as a snake would.

COW TONGUE
Opuntia linguiformis

This cactus can range from three to five feet tall and reminds many of the shape of a cow's tongue. These cacti can't be missed in our garden, especially in April and early May when they're covered in ombré blooms in yellows and pinks.

BRITTLEBUSH
Encelia farinosa

This is a shrub native to California. Its branches are brittle and burst forth in daisy-like yellow flowers. In the superbloom of 2017, the low desert landscape was covered in yellow blooms from this bush.

CENTURY PLANT
Agave americana

This is a type of agave native to the southwestern United States and Mexico. At the end of its life (at around twenty to thirty years old) the plant utilizes the last of its energy to grow an impressive stalk and bloom. When we first moved to Joshua Tree, our garden had a fully matured agave that grew a twenty-foot stalk within a matter of months. We watched the process in awe— once the mother plant died, the stalk released new century plant seeds, completing the circle of life.

OCOTILLO
Fouquieria splendens

This plant is native to the southwestern United States and can grow to a height of thirty feet. For parts of the year, it looks like dried sticks with thorns, but after a little rain or watering it will grow leaves and turn green.

Indoor Plant Guide

EUPHORBIA

These plants are often mistaken for cacti, but are in fact their own genus that range in size from very small to the size of trees. To spot the difference between a cactus and a euphorbia, take a look at the spines or thorns. If it has areoles (clusters of spines or fibers), then it is a cactus. A euphorbia's thorns grow directly out of the stem and usually appear in pairs. When punctured or cut, euphorbias let out a white milky residue called latex that is meant to keep predators away. If it gets on your skin, you should rinse it off immediately since it may cause irritation. Some of our favorites are *Euphorbia tirucalli*, *Euphorbia lactea*, *Euphorbia ingens*, and *Euphorbia ammak*.

POTHOS

This is a beautiful leaf-growing vine that is extremely durable. They are very easy to grow and are best in indirect sunlight. Their vines can reach twenty to forty feet long. We love using pothos in spots where their vines can hang over a wall or down from a suspended macramé planter.

MARANTA (PRAYER PLANT)

Maranta leuconeura

This leafy plant doesn't like direct sunlight. When we first put one in our house, we thought it wasn't doing well during the day, but each night it would perk up into a very happy-looking plant. As the night goes on, you can watch the plant leaves move and start to face upward.

PRICKLY PEAR CACTI
Opuntia

These cacti are great for small to medium pots inside. They're usually hardy and adapt well to most environments. We like using them as accent plants, but are careful to make sure that they aren't in a pathway where people will get stuck to them.

PENCIL CACTUS
Euphorbia tirucalli

This is actually a euphorbia; its common name is a misnomer. Originally from Africa, it has pencil-size branches and can grow up to twenty feet tall outdoors and six feet indoors. There are no thorns, which makes it especially great for indoor use. We have one in our dining area and love how its pencil arms fill the corner.

Gardening with Cacti and Euphorbias

When we moved to Joshua Tree, we brought our most prized possession with us: a six-foot-tall *Euphorbia trigona*. We've become particularly attached to this lucky euphorbia that stands proudly in our living room and welcomes us home each day. Our movers were disgruntled about taking this six-foot spiny plant down the state of California, especially when they saw our cactus garden in Joshua Tree. They wondered why we would ever need *another* cactus.

Our answer was that this plant was like our baby and, of course, having plants inside a home is a very different, but equally important, experience to being with plants outdoors.

CACTUS PLANTING GUIDE

Our favorite times of day for planting outdoors are early morning or dusk. Not only are these both beautiful parts of the day to be outside, but they're also much more forgiving weather-wise (particularly in the summer months).

Method

PREPARATION Put on your gardening gloves, and wrap your cactus in brown paper (this helps to avoid getting any cactus spines on you as you're planting). Use a pocketknife to slice a seam down the side of the plastic pot as well as around the bottom edge.

You'll Need

A roll of brown paper

Pocketknife

Cactus soil

Shovel (*for outdoor planting*)

Planter (*for indoor planting*)

A friend

Gardening gloves

DIG If you're planting outside, dig a hole about twice the size of the pot it was previously in. If you're planting indoors, make sure that your pot is larger than its current container if you'd like it to continue growing. (You can purposely stunt the growth of your cactus if it's already too tall for your space by keeping it in a smaller planter.)

PLANT Sprinkle the bottom of your freshly dug hole or planter with cactus and succulent soil. Planting large cacti is typically a two-person job, so you'll want to have a friend help at this point. Have one person lift the sliced container while the other person holds the cactus wrapped in paper to prevent any breakage.

Once the cactus is upright, removed the sliced container and fill the hole back up with sand from the surrounding land. For indoor planting, you'll want to remove the container first before placing the cactus in its pot, and fill in with cactus soil.

ADD ROCKS We love gardening with rocks both indoors and out. Outdoors, we suggest gathering large rocks and organically arranging them around your cacti. Indoors, we love to cover over our cactus soil with small collected rocks in uniform color palettes. This not only looks beautiful, but mimics the landscape around us.

WATER Flood your plant (aka your new friend) with water to help remove air pockets from the soil, and allow your plant to adjust to its new home.

Wait a couple of weeks before watering your cactus again. We water our indoor cacti every 2 weeks, while we have our irrigation system set to water our outdoor plants every other day. Fully exposed to the harsh sun, outdoor cacti generally need more water than indoor ones.

Sunrise

We woke early and stumbled out into the darkness with a flashlight to guide our way. Typically the full moon acts as daylight—enough to see the landscape ahead—but this moon was different. As our eyes adjusted, we looked to the sky and all at once saw the stars, the lunar eclipse, and the sun rising behind us.

The first glimpses of morning light are a cue for some wildlife to go back to sleep, while others rise. Some days, coyotes act as our alarm clock, yipping to celebrate as the sun comes up. Whether it's a stream of light that floods our bedroom or the exuberance of coyotes that wakes us, this is the true beginning to each day. Though we've always been morning people, we've never felt more encouraged to get out of bed with the rising sun than we do here in the desert. Our day has shifted forward in time to make the most of daylight hours and to be able to catch two stunning shows each day: sunrise and sunset.

As the shifting sunlight eases us into the day, we use this time to start fresh with a simple meditation or smudging. Keeping a clean and clear home helps our minds find clarity as well. This repetitive practice of doing the same thing at the same time each day keeps us from overthinking and provides us with a simple way to grow. Though we have been taught to have a linear life, we've learned there is no such thing. Our lives rotate in cycles much like the sun, and we've found that keeping ourselves connected to these cycles simply feels natural.

A FOCUS ON BREATH

◆ ◆ ◆

Aleksandra Zee is a close friend of ours who spends her time between the Mojave Desert and Oakland, California. Much of her practice as a woodworker is inspired by the natural hues and open landscape of Joshua Tree, removed from distraction. Her home in the city reflects this as well, as she surrounds herself with a curated selection of objects that inspire her. The simplicity and organization of her home leave her more space to focus on breath, meditation, and simple morning rituals.

Before heading to her studio, Aleksandra starts her mornings off slowly with a meditation on a daybed cushion in her living room, with the sun streaming in. Even with her studio practice consistently increasing in pace, her life at home has become slower and more intentional. While it's normal for an increase in projects to build up anxiety, Aleksandra accepts and settles her anxieties by focusing on her breath. Breath is basic to life, and by creating a morning ritual around it, she sets intentions for daily breathing patterns.

There's a comfort to be found in the ordinary. Like a tried-and-true recipe (think mashed potatoes or lasagna), sometimes it's those simple classics that bring the most warmth. Before beginning the practice below, remember that life is only as complicated as we make it. Beginning each day by returning to the simplest form of life—our breath—is such a beautiful reminder of that.

Guided Sunrise Meditation

SPACE

Find a quiet corner at home that brings you joy. If you feel there is no such corner, create one. To start, maybe this simply means clearing a space in the corner of your bedroom for a floor cushion, a favorite plant, and a candle. Each day when you wake up, let this space you've created become a reminder to begin today's meditation practice. You may also consider creating a nonverbal signal to others you live with so they know you're meditating and are aware not to interrupt. For example, you could sit facing a particular window or on a cushion reserved for your meditation practice.

TIME

It's normal for our minds to wander during meditation, and one of the easiest places to wander is wondering how long it's been or what time it is. Setting a timer on your phone for however long you'd like to meditate—whether it's ten minutes, thirty minutes, or an hour—sets you free from worrying about time restrictions. Personally, we use the "chimes" tone that comes on the iPhone's clock app (under timer).

SETTLE

Cross your legs or let your feet touch the floor, and find comfort in the simplicity of sitting. Adjust your posture to a place of strength and comfort. Allow your arms to rest gently, and remind yourself how special it is to give yourself this time to just be.

SOFTEN

Soften your gaze, and begin to focus on your other senses. What sounds do you hear in and around your home? Appreciate and accept everything you hear as a part of your experience. Notice how your body feels—whether it's tense or relaxed—and accept its current state.

BELIEVE

Believe in the power of belief. This is your time to believe that today will be beautiful, powerful, productive…whatever you dream it to be. We all have the opportunity to manifest our thoughts and dreams.

ENVISION

Close your eyes fully, and envision an open yet dimly lit desert landscape before you. Breathe in through your nose and out through your mouth for ten breaths while you take in this beautiful scene. For every breath in, accept personal imperfections and the anxieties that work and life bring. For every breath out, release those anxieties.

After ten breaths, envision a small light at the horizon. Now as you breathe in, accept the light of this new day, and as you breathe out again, allow the light to expand. As you breathe in and out, and the light expands further and further across the sky, imagine the warmth of this light on your skin. The more warmth you feel, the more anxieties are accepted and released. If your mind wanders, gently nudge yourself back to the rising sun and vision of a calm desert landscape.

MANIFEST

Once the light of the sun completely fills the sky and you cannot imagine the light spreading any further, slowly open your eyes and notice how you now feel. No matter where you live, you can bring this breath and warmth of the desert sun with you through the rest of your day.

For Aleksandra, this means headphones and instrumental music that guide her through her art practice. Some days, she's able to find a creative flow that makes her feel as though her body is moving without a concrete thought of doing so. This does not mean that all days will be perfect and uninterrupted hours of meditation, but on some days that creative flow will be found. That alone is plenty to be grateful for.

Aleksandra's Suggestions for a Calm Home

EXPLORE A MUTED COLOR PALETTE

Simplifying the color palette of your home can bring incredible calm to your space. For Aleksandra, this means a lot of white with natural materials such as linen, wood, and leathers in rich browns.

Wooden artwork by Aleksandra Zee

KEEP THINGS FRESH

Our lives are constantly evolving, and so our homes should be too. Aleksandra often switches out plates, ceramics, and textiles to keep her home feeling inspirational. In turn, this motivates her to keep her space clean and organized.

CURATE POSSESSIONS

Consider function before form. Everything in Aleksandra's home is either functional or sentimental. She freely donates and sells items that aren't serving a purpose in her home, which keeps her space clutter-free.

FIND A PLACE FOR EVERYTHING

An organized home can visually represent the calm in our minds. Aleksandra finds that an organized home opens her to the freedom of meditation.

JUNIPER CLEANSE

The silence of sunrise reminds us to check in with our personal health both mentally and physically. For thousands of years, aromatic plant smoke has been practically utilized to purify the air by greatly reducing airborne bacteria. Catering to the health of our bodies affects the health of our minds, creating a fresh start to the day. Cleansing with plant smoke—also known as smudging—can be done with many types of herbs.

For sunrise though, our preferred plant to burn is California juniper—one of our favorite trees native to the Mojave. Its trunk twists upward to a scaly evergreen with whitish-blue berries dotting the surface. It's a beautiful plant that can be found in the higher elevations of Joshua Tree National Park and the surrounding high desert. Smudging with this plant at home offers us a fresh start to each day and a clear mind.

If you'd like to practice this at home, think about what herbal plants are native to your area that can also be sustainably foraged. Maybe this means starting a small herbal garden of your own in your kitchen or outside if you have land of your own.

You'll Need

Spool of cotton string (*No synthetics, but this can be any natural string that calls to you.*)

Scissors

Bunch of herbs (*In this case we're using California juniper.*)

Method

GATHER Begin by gathering or sustainably foraging a handful of your herb or plant of choice. Here we're using juniper, but rosemary, sage, and lavender work great as well. Cut the herbs to the length you'd like your final smudge stick to be—we recommend around 6 inches. Always remember not to forage from national parks and to be considerate of each plant when taking a clipping. If it doesn't feel right to forage from a particular plant, offer the plant some water and move on to an alternative.

WRAP Cut a 5-foot strand of cotton or natural string (this can be any color you'd like). Neatly bundle your freshly cut herbs, and starting from the stems of your bundle, begin to tightly wrap upward at a diagonal. We like to keep our strings evenly spaced as we do this. Once you reach the top of the bundle, reverse your way down, mindfully crossing over your previous strings to create x's. At the bottom of the bundle, tie a small knot to complete the wrapping.

TRIM Now that your bundle is wrapped, you can go back in with your scissors to trim and clean up the herbs if there are any areas that don't seem as secure or are simply too long for the bundle.

DRY Allow your freshly bundled herbs to dry out for 1–2 weeks in a space such as a windowsill.

BURN Once fully dry, hold a match to the end of your smudge stick until it creates a flame. Allow the juniper to burn for a few moments before blowing it out. Aromatic smoke will flow from the end of your bundle, cleansing the air around you. Slowly breathe in and out as you move through your home, allowing the smoke to billow into every corner. As you do this, imagine the smoke engulfing any negativity you or your home has experienced. Welcome a fresh start to the day, both mentally and physically.

Morning

We woke to
moody skies
and snowcapped
mountains in the
distance and set out
on an adventure
to find snow for
ourselves. We drove
up in elevation
until we reached
Pioneertown
Mountains Preserve,
where the white
sky thickened and
faded into the sandy
landscape before us.
It was there that we
found magic.

As soon as the sun radiates an even glow over the landscape, the day is prompted to begin. Morning is the most hopeful time of day—a chance to start slow and set the tone for every moment that follows. We love the ritual of morning coffee or tea and have found making it to be just as enjoyable as the act of drinking it.

Mornings also tend to be when our bodies feel driest. In this place devoid of water, we're ironically reminded of it often. In order to help conserve resources while keeping ourselves hydrated and healthy, we look to morning recipes and rituals with multitasking abilities. This means teas with the ability to keep us healthy and hydrated longer and rearranging the order of everyday acts to increase the humidity inside our home.

SLOWING DOWN

◆◆◆

Slow morning rituals are sweet reminders that busy days do not necessarily make meaningful ones. The desert has taught us to multitask in the laziest of ways so that each moment can be slowed down while still accomplishing our goals. Staying healthy—both mentally and physically—is on the top of that list. Starting the day with a clear mind means we're automatically given more time to create what we want to create, without the need to rush a moment of it.

As the first golden rays of sun begin to fill our kitchen, we feel energized to start the day. This usually means brewing up a warm beverage (particularly in the cooler months). We especially love the Golden Milk Tea on the following page, created by our favorite local restaurant La Copine, with its dual function of taking care of our bodies while relishing the moment.

Restaurant owners Claire Wadsworth and Nikki Hill created this turmeric tea simply to keep their staff healthy, but it quickly became a menu item. As soon as you walk into their restaurant situated amidst the open desert landscape, you can feel a warm and communal energy. It's very clear that every offering they develop for our desert community is made with love. This tea is no exception and serves as a reminder that mental and physical health can be achieved simultaneously. We so admire the beautiful community they've created by slowly growing their business with a focus on their own personal happiness, as well as the happiness of those around them.

The next time you feel in need of a healthy boost, try the tea recipe below. This tea is especially efficacious during flu season, as turmeric helps to fight inflammation as well as colds. Claire and Nikki suggest enjoying it with a homemade English muffin with butter and jam or three to five Sun Salutations to begin your day.

LA COPINE'S GOLDEN MILK TEA

Method

COMBINE In a large pot combine the water, turmeric, and ginger. Squeeze and drop the lemon halves into the pot.

MAKE A SACHET Gently smash* the cardamom pods and cinnamon sticks. Make a sachet* with the cardamom, cinnamon, cloves, black pepper, rosemary, and thyme.

SIMMER Add the sachet to the pot, cover with a lid, and bring to a low boil. Lower the heat, tilt the lid, allowing steam to escape, and simmer for 45 minutes.

STEEP Remove the pot from heat, fully cover, and let steep for 1–2 hours. Using tongs, squeeze the lemons and sachet, then discard. Strain the liquid through a chinois* into another pot or mixing vessel. Whisk in the coconut milk and honey until smooth.

STORE Store in lidded glass jars and keep refrigerated. This makes a golden milk concentrate that will stay good for up to 2 weeks.

ENJOY To enjoy a cup of golden milk, all you have to do is pour 2–3 ounces of the concentrate (stir before using) into a mug, add 2–3 ounces of your preferred milk, and top off with freshly boiled water. To make an iced golden milk, add cold water and pour over ice.

You'll Need

A large pot

Chinois (or other strainer)

Cheesecloth

Kitchen string

Tongs

Whisk

Glass jars for storing concentrate

6 cups water

3 ounces organic ground turmeric

½ cup gingerroot, peeled and sliced

Organic lemon, sliced in half

5 green cardamom pods

1 cinnamon stick

6 cloves

½ teaspoon black peppercorns

2 sprigs rosemary

7 sprigs thyme

1 can coconut milk, full fat

½ cup honey

---

*smash: cardamom pods and cinnamon sticks can be crushed by using the back of your knife or the bottom of a pot

*sachet: made by wrapping cheesecloth entirely around spices and herbs then tied with kitchen string

*chinois: a superfine mesh strainer, but you can also use a cheesecloth-lined strainer

After enjoying this tea, you will understand why "Happy Place in the Universe" has a permanent place in Claire and Nikki's minds, as though it sits under La Copine's sign, by Kris Chau, outside their restaurant. Our hope is that you will feel similar contentment as you enjoy this tea at home.

If you feel inspired after making this tea, try experimenting with other desert ingredients. Some ideas to get started include mesquite, Mormon tea, piñon pine, creosote, apricots, cactus, pistachios, sweet limes, citrus, chile peppers, juniper, dates, and prunes. Keep in mind that desert foraging is best done from your land to protect our desert resources, and always remember to safely identify foraged plants as edible before consuming them.

La Copine's Garde Manger cook Sarah Witt created High Desert Test Kitchen, which is also an incredible source of inspiration for creating recipes with ingredients native to the desert. You can find more information about this in our resource guide at the back of this book.

"Cooking without a recipe is like cooking from the soul."

—Claire and Nikki
of La Copine

SLOW DRIP COFFEE

The sound of grinding coffee beans and the slow drip of a Chemex romanticize our mornings here in the desert. Making drip coffee is a beautiful sensory experience, and taking in all of the sounds, the smell, and the warmth of the coffee wakes us up quite possibly more than the caffeine itself.

Our friend Casey Goch has inspired us with a passion for coffee that reaches far beyond the bean itself. After moving to Los Angeles, she began drinking coffee as a way to connect with a new community. She found coffee to be an experience and a means to enjoy the simple moments in life. Inspired by coffee's ability to bring people together, she started Shreebs, a coffee company based on human connection. Coffee is meant to be served alongside brainstorms, new friendships, and sunrises with loved ones.

One of Casey's most adored rituals while camping in Joshua Tree is a morning campfire. Making coffee while camping requires

You'll Need

Paper filter

Chemex

Grinder

Organic coffee beans
(*2 tablespoons for each 8-ounce cup*)

Kettle of boiling water

Spoon

a little more effort, but in turn the process and ritual add to the enjoyment of the experience. Grinding the beans with a hand grinder, filling the stovetop percolator, and setting it on the fire to wait patiently offer time for conversation.

No matter whether you find yourself indoors or out on any given morning, pour-over coffee is a really wonderful way to begin each day. For single servings, try a V60 dripper, or for a larger batch for a group try a Chemex. Removing machinery from the process and brewing coffee by hand provide time and space in the most natural way.

Method   TOTAL TIME: 4 MINUTES

BOIL Bring water to a boil (include an extra 4 ounces of water for preheating).

PREPARE Set a paper filter in the Chemex funnel with the multiedge side toward the spout.

PREHEAT Pour hot water in a circular motion to completely saturate the filter and preheat the glass. Empty the water from the preheat. (It's okay to leave the filter in place.)

GRIND Grind 2 tablespoons of coffee for each 8 ounces of water you plan to use (example: 4 tablespoons = 2 cups).

BLOOM Place the grounds in the Chemex filter and level off. Pour the hot water in a circular or zigzag motion to saturate all the grounds.

STIR Use a spoon to mix, making sure there are no dry clumps of coffee, and then wait (45 seconds).

BREW Begin pouring the water again, slowly and evenly, until all of your water is gone (60 seconds). Let the water run through completely, and then discard the filter.

ENJOY Pour the coffee into your favorite mugs, find a cozy spot in the house, and enjoy with friends and family.

THE RITUAL OF HYDRATION

❖ ❖ ❖

To say the least, moving to the desert has been transformative to life as we previously knew it. While yes, it can often sound romantic, life here has simultaneously been the hardest and most rewarding times we've yet to experience. We've learned through a series of mistakes and firsts—life without the conveniences that a city offers, being responsible not only for doing our work but creating our work, building and maintaining property, and learning how the harsh climate here can throw any of those things out of whack in an instant. Life in the desert has been a test of patience and strength that has allowed us to grow beyond the years we spent living in cities. It's reinforced how very small we are, how powerful nature is, and our desire to be in some small way more connected to all of it.

Completely unplanned, we made the move from San Francisco to Joshua Tree at the same time as our good friends Tienlyn Jacobson and Nikko DeTranquilli. We've been on a similar path of resistance for the past couple of years, checking in with each other along the way through renovation projects and sandstorms. Through the process, we've all learned from and been inspired by the resilience of the plants and animals that live here, and their adaptation to the extreme temperatures and arid climate. We feel stronger than ever, but ultimately our conversations often lead to the basis of all life: water.

Spend a period of time in the desert, and you'll find rain suddenly feels sacred. For us, it's become a reminder to stop and enjoy the moment—the sound, the feel, the smell of it all. While we typically only get a few rainstorms per year, the smell of our native creosote plants when wet has become a sentimental scent. Though the dry climate and high elevation here are great for many things—drying laundry, drying fruits, drying anything

really—it's caused considerable adjustments for our bodies. Self-care has become a gift, and over time we've learned more ways to increase hydration while still being conscious of desert resources. We feel incredibly grateful to live in the desert in a time where we have access to water, but also understand that the water supply here is far from endless.

While morning routines can be beautiful, they easily become daunting with too many additions. Inspired by Tienlyn and Nikko, the morning hydration ritual below is rooted in simplicity and utilizes a drought-tolerant superfood called moringa to assist in moisture retainment. From seeds (readily available online), Nikko grows moringa on their property here in Joshua Tree. This incredible plant doesn't need much water—it utilizes its minimal resources wisely by reserving as much as possible. This plant can offer our bodies the same conservation, providing up a ritual essential to our well-being.

A Cup of Tea

Tea is a wonderful way to begin the day for hydration benefits, but to retain as much of that water as possible, moringa is a really great option. Moringa is native to parts of Africa and Asia and allows your body to retain hydration with roughly three times the amount of potassium as a banana. It's been known to help with focus, energy, digestion, migraines, and has antiaging characteristics. It's loaded with nutrients, including protein, vitamin B6, vitamin C, and iron, making it seem almost too good to be true.

We've found the flavor to be subtle and earthy. It works just as well simply mixed with hot water as it does in an almond milk latte. You can purchase moringa in powder, oil, or seed form—if you'd like to try growing the plant yourself to enjoy the fresh leaves, which are similar to arugula.

MORINGA TEA

Method

Scoop the moringa powder into your favorite mug. Allow your boiled water to cool to drinking temperature before pouring it over the moringa powder to fill your mug (using boiling water risks breaking down the enzymes and reduces nutritional benefits of the moringa). Stir the powder into the hot water until fully blended.

You'll Need

½ teaspoon moringa powder *(Be cautious not to use much more than this, as it can act as a natural laxative.)*

1 cup hot water

Spoon

MORINGA LATTE

Method

Scoop the moringa powder into your favorite mug, and pour the warmed almond milk over the top to fill. Whisk the powder into the warmed almond milk until fully blended.

You'll Need

½ teaspoon moringa powder

1 cup warmed almond milk

Small whisk

Shower

The morning ritual of a shower is a great time to practice gratitude for access to clean water, particularly in our dry landscape. Tie a bundle of creosote and eucalyptus to your showerhead for the smell of desert rain, as we suggest in our third design mantra: Design for Ordinary Experiences.

MOISTURIZE

Reordering daily routines has the ability to make each part of the process more productive and meaningful. Try applying lotion while your body is still wet to hold in the moisture of your shower, and pat your skin dry afterward. Your skin will absorb extra hydration while avoiding a shiny residue that lotions can sometimes create.

Think of the body butter and face mask recipes below as a morning ritual. Once moisturizing becomes a daily habit, good results will manifest.

MORINGA BODY BUTTER

This recipe is a simplified version of a lotion recipe that Tienlyn has used for years.

Method

HEAT AND COMBINE Combine the oils, shea butter, and beeswax in a double boiler. If you don't have a double boiler, a glass bowl secured above a pot of boiling water works great too. If using this method, make sure there are air gaps on the sides of the bowl so steam has a place to escape to. This can be done by securing a wooden spoon to the underside of each side of the bowl. As the ingredients begin to melt, stir to combine.

ADD ESSENTIAL OILS AND MORINGA Add the lemon verbena essential oil to soften skin and retain moisture. The soothing smell also works to calm and ease anxiety. As the oils start to cool, add the moringa powder for additional antiaging benefits.

STORE Pour the liquid ingredients into a mason jar or tin and store at room temperature to solidify. Keep the body butter in your shower as a reminder to apply right after showering.

You'll Need

1 fluid ounce argan oil (*Almond oil or jojoba oil will work as well.*)

1 fluid ounce chaparral oil (*Native to the Mojave, this oil keeps skin glowing in the harshest environments. We get ours from La Abeja Herbs, listed in our Resource Guide at the back of this book.*)

½ cup coconut oil

3 tablespoons shea butter or cocoa butter

¼ cup beeswax

Therapeutic-grade lemon verbena (*several drops according to preference*)

½ tablespoon moringa powder

A glass jar

SIMPLE MORNING FACE MASK

This recipe is purposely simple. The fewer ingredients necessary, the more likely you are to actually use this mask regularly—which is where a lot of the true benefits start to kick in. The base of this mask is honey, which retains moisture while acting as an antibacterial agent. That also makes it a great way to combat acne without overdrying your skin. The moringa powder contains zeatin, a plant hormone linked to antiaging, which will help with dry skin, fine lines and wrinkles, and premature aging.

Method

COMBINE Stir the honey and moringa powder together until fully combined. If you have an extra avocado lying around, you can also add ¼ of it to the mixture for additional moisture, especially for flaky skin or dry patches.

APPLY Apply the mask to your face, neck, and décolletage for 10–15 minutes. (Wear a low-cut shirt or towel while applying this mask to your décolletage, as it can get messy.)

RINSE Start by wetting your hands and massaging the mask in small, gentle circles, adding water as you go to remove the mask slowly. Removing the mask this way helps keep the moringa grain on your face until the very end to help with exfoliation.

You'll Need

1 teaspoon of raw and/or organic honey (*Better yet, buy it from your local farmers' market.*)

½ teaspoon moringa

¼ avocado (*optional*)

Humidify Naturally

It's possible to humidify your space with ordinary acts—leave your shower door open after showering, skip the bathroom fan, let the kettle go a little longer, and dry intimates and small laundry items indoors. The excess moisture or steam from each of these acts will gratifyingly increase the humidity of the air around you without the use of additional water. If you're curious whether the air in your home is at a healthy humidity, the average suggested range for health and comfort is between 40 and 50 percent.

The most important thing to remember here is to make a habit of these small acts. It's the repetition that will make an impact on the humidity of your home over time.

VISUAL CUES

For three years total, and during her first couple of years living in Joshua Tree, Tienlyn struggled with interstitial cystitis. She tried everything from antibiotics, vitamins, and diet adjustments to holistic remedies, and nothing seemed to help. After her doctor recommended taking daily antibiotics, she knew there had to be a better way. She finally turned to water as the solution. As soon as she began drinking a 2.2-liter bottle of water daily, her symptoms disappeared completely. Tienlyn's story goes to show how powerful hydration truly is. Water is a life source, but can also act as a remedy for some illnesses.

Method

Give yourself a visual representation of how much water to drink in a day by filling a 2.2-liter reusable bottle. Make it your personal goal to drink through the entire bottle each day, and carry your water supply with you as a reminder. This visual helps with maintaining a mindful approach to hydration, while not overutilizing our desert resources.

To make a simple glass of water extra enjoyable, eat a raw moringa seed (just the white interior of the seed) just before drinking. The remnants of the seed will make the water taste sweet and feel extra silky. Make sure not to eat more than a couple of moringa seeds at a time though, as they also act as a natural laxative.

Midday

Just before the new year on a quiet hike with family on Barker Dam Trail, we rounded a bend in the path to be greeted by the most enchanting creature. A bighorn sheep stood confidently before us, climbing straight up boulders without a second thought. We silently watched him gracefully navigate piles of rocks and hoped by proximity that we would gain just a fraction of this confident energy as we entered the next year.

Midday in the desert is a time we often overlook, but it feels most authentic to life here. The sun is at its harshest point, casting strong shadows from the Joshua trees that remind us of all of the other intense contrasts here—of life, climate, and terrain.

The middle of the day is when we work the hardest. It's during this time that our bodies and minds get tired and are later rewarded with sunset. Particularly during the summer months, the sun beats down on all life here, testing plants and animals on their abilities to survive with little water. To survive here requires resiliency, a quality we admire. At times, everything is a little harder out here—instant satisfaction has dissolved, and we're continually tested by the desert's extreme weather, although our time here has also consisted of some of the most serene days we've yet to experience. This contrast has made us feel stronger and more connected to our environment.

Midday varies greatly through the seasons. In the summer, you'll find us either opting for shade while working inside or soaking in our cowboy tub for a quick break. In this dry climate, it's incredible how much a little bit of water can cool us down. In cooler months, we find ourselves out hiking trails in Joshua Tree National Park and taking in the details of this beautiful landscape.

NATURAL ABSTRACTION

❖ ❖ ❖

Often as we hike through Joshua Tree National Park, we're reminded of the work of our close friend and abstract painter Heather Day. Heather often suggests, "If you don't understand abstraction, take a look at the natural world that surrounds us." She's particularly drawn to water and observes the organic contours of the coast and washes of blues while home in San Francisco. When she's here in Joshua Tree, the lack of water is immediately apparent, but signs of water's influence are all around. Elegant lines carved by water and wind flow through the boulders, and sand is sculpted into washes that mimic the movement of water itself.

While exploring different areas of Joshua Tree, you'll also find a beautiful variety of colors in the rocks, texture in the dried roots of desert senna and cholla skeletons, patterns in the cacti and Joshua trees, and boulders of incredible proportions.

Through her paintings, Heather translates the sounds and feelings of her environment conversationally onto a surface through texture, color, and other elements of abstraction. She seamlessly blends the senses and wonders if a texture is fast or slow or if forms are playful or serious.

We've taken many walks through Joshua Tree together, and of all those moments it's the ordinary ones that we remember most vividly. Stepping on a round stone as it sinks into the earth below our feet is oddly satisfying, and—lucky us—there are so many of those oddly satisfying moments to be found out in nature.

CURIOSITY IN THE ORDINARY

Yearly check-ins and goals are wonderful, but considering that our days are the foundation of our years, daily check-ins are incredibly important as well. Midday is a great time to pause and reflect both personally and with work.

Take a moment in the middle of your day to stop and notice your current environment. Separate your mind from the categories you've placed on things and see them for what they are. We've found that encouraging ourselves to stay curious about the details of our surroundings functions as the perfect refresh, and the addition of fresh air further awakens our creative minds. Use the trail guide that follows as a reference for a midday hike, and as a way to refresh and find abstraction in nature.

Season

As with all hikes in Joshua Tree, it's only recommended to take this trail in spring, fall, and winter months (particularly if you plan to go midday, the summer months in Joshua Tree are too harsh for hiking).

Abstraction immediately confronts us as we enter the Barker Dam Trail—boulders surround us in surreal forms not usually found in the physical world. In contrast to other trails in the park, this trail in particular has many signs of water's influence. Not only have the boulders themselves been rounded and carved by water over millions of years, but this trail is one of the few in the park that leads to water itself. Even before you reach the dam, you'll notice water's influence with a greater variety of plants growing optimistically from rock crevices.

Trail

Barker Dam, Joshua Tree National Park

(Check the trail guide section of this book for more information on this trail.)

What to Bring

Backpack

2 bottles of water, one for drinking, one for painting

Sunscreen

Sunglasses or hat *(if you don't want sunglasses to affect the way you see color and light)*

Sketchbook

Toolbox

Pencils

Pastels

Brushes

Acrylic paint

Tape

Eraser

Mood

Rather than focusing on speed or athleticism during this hike, allow it to be playful. Slowly enter the trail and pay attention to the mood around you. As you come across textures, do they feel fast or slow? If you were to draw it, would you draw it quickly or methodically?

Listen to the sounds around you. How do they relate to the landscape? The desert has a tendency to be extremely quiet, which allows the varying boulder formations and contrast of the cyan sky to take center stage. The rocks and plants here are not as quiet as their environment, with clear signs suggesting that we find a balance between interaction and distance. The surrounding boulders are textured and playful, inviting us to engage. As an especially playful national park, rock climbing is encouraged here—movement itself sparks creativity, and climbing up the boulders we feel refreshed. Meanwhile, the bold personalities of the surrounding cacti and sharp plants caution us to keep our distance.

In nature we have less control, but that's okay. We walk around boulders or plants that have decided their home is at the center of the trail. It puts us at ease accepting and admiring these natural imperfections. There's nothing to fix here; it's one place where we can enjoy everything just as it is.

Contrast

At midday our shadows are sharp and blunt, reminding us of our presence and our relationship to the surrounding environment. Shadows on boulders and plants enunciate their form.

As we continue down the trail, we're reminded of contrast once again. In the desert, our focus on water itself becomes heightened. Once we reach the dam, increased plant life makes the lack of water before it even more apparent. Still, most of the plants hug to the boulders, in hopes of collecting increased rainwater runoff.

In these intersections of plants and boulders, the variation between them informs and allows us to see more detail in each element. Dried roots of California buckwheat feel loud and hectic in comparison to the speckled monzogranite boulder next to it. The contrast of the root's cool tones brings out an increased warmth in the boulder's coloring.

With an open horizon, our awareness of the sky increases as well. In stark contrast, the peach boulder formations draw a clean line against a cyan sky. Especially at Barker Dam, the sky's blue wash takes over the landscape as it is reflected by the water.

Repetition

The water of the dam acts as a mirror and repeats not only the sky, but also the rocks and plants as well. Standing at the water's edge, we wonder how we would translate these abstract forms into a painting.

Form

Abstraction is about breaking down the landscape or environment before us into its purest form. It's important to zoom in, and take some time to study one plant or rock from all sides. How does each side make you feel or see?

Space

The negative spaces between boulders are reminders of what's there just as much as what's not. The shapes of these negative spaces teach us about the massive scale of the boulders themselves and the weight that they must hold. We wonder how to translate a form with such weight in contrast to a similar shape of negative space onto paper.

With every turn in the trail, we find more evidence of where water has been. Watermarks on rocks are reminders of the transformation of space through time and the weight of the stories that this landscape holds.

Method

Now that you have observed your landscape, find a spot to sit with your sketchbook. Sit, observe, and paint what you see. Meditate on the elements you've seen: the mood, contrast, repetition, form, and space.

If you still feel as though you don't understand abstraction enough to paint it, remember Heather's words again: "It's all around you."

TRAIL GUIDE

◆◆◆

ALWAYS REMEMBER TO LEAVE NO TRACE: TAKE ONLY PHOTOGRAPHS, LEAVE ONLY FOOTPRINTS, PACK OUT WHAT YOU PACK IN, AND STAY ON DESIGNATED TRAILS TO HELP PRESERVE THE FRAGILE ECOSYSTEM.

We never know quite where to begin with our recommendations for hikes in Joshua Tree as there's a little bit of everything here—epic boulders, strange plants, and landscapes that simply feel alien. With over 1,200 square miles of rock formations, Joshua trees, native cacti, hiking trails, and winding roads, this landscape is open for endless exploration. We've shared just a few of our favorite trails below, but there's always more to discover.

Keep in mind that the following trails are best enjoyed during winter, spring, and fall. Remember to bring plenty of water and pack sunscreen year-round. Turn around and head back home once your water supply is half gone, no matter what.

North View Trail

This is one of the first trails you'll find when entering Joshua Tree National Park from the west. Full of beauty, here you'll find incredible rock formations, Joshua trees, and wide-open views facing north toward Joshua Tree and Twentynine Palms.

How to Access

Access this trail through the west entrance of Joshua Tree National Park. Drive about 1.2 miles in, and park your car just before mile marker 24 on the left-hand side. (You'll see a small parking lot for about four cars.)

The beginning of the trail is not incredibly well marked, but it's easy to find if you know what to look for. Hike straight into the wash until you see trailhead signs. Turn right at these signs, and go a short way until you find a sign for North View Trail, at which point you will go left.

For this trail we would also recommend that you bring your phone and/or a map. There are a couple spots throughout the trail where it can be easy to wonder, "is this still it?" Luckily, this trail is not too far into the park so it's still possible to get cell service. Use your phone or map to make sure that you're still headed in the right direction.

Trail Info

- 6.5-mile loop
- about 3–4 hours

Hidden Valley

This is one of our favorite trails since it gives a great overview of the park and is good for all ages—we've even taken grandparents on it! There are many Joshua trees, local plants, and boulders to scramble on. The trail itself is fairly level and only takes about one hour to hike. However, if you decide to explore boulders along the trail, this can become a half-day adventure.

How to Access

Use the west entrance of the park and drive about 9.1 miles before leaving your car at the Hidden Valley parking and picnic area. Find the trail entrance right off the parking lot.

Trail Info

- 1-mile loop
- about 45 minutes to 1 hour to hike

Barker Dam

This trail is particularly full of life, as it's one of the few places to find water. Depending on the time of year and the amount of recent rainfall, the dam can be completely full of water. It was originally constructed in 1900 by CO Barker and then built higher by Bill Keys in 1949 to store water for irrigation and cattle. These days, it's a picturesque hike with many types of vegetation such as piñon pine, juniper, manzanita, and Joshua trees, as well as beautiful rock formations. There's even an area toward the end of the trail with petroglyphs drawn by Native Americans. The dam is a great place to watch for wildlife like bighorn sheep.

How to Access

Use the west entrance and drive about nine miles into the park. Turn left on Barker Dam Road and follow the signs to the trail for another 1.5 miles. The trail is just off of the parking area.

Trail Info

- 1.5-mile loop
- about 45 minutes to hike

Ryan Mountain

This is one of the more challenging hikes in the park with an elevation gain of around 1,060 feet. Upon reaching the summit, you'll be rewarded with expansive views of the Joshua trees and rock formations.

How to Access

Use the west entrance and drive about 12.7 miles into the park. Turn right into the Ryan Mountain parking area. The trail is immediately off of the parking area.

Trail Info

- 2.9 miles round-trip
- about 1.5 hours to hike

Willow Hole Trail

This is a moderate hike through mostly sandy washes and rock formations. About 1.2 miles down the trail you'll arrive at the Willow Hole trailhead. The trail dead-ends at Willow Hole where there is an abundance of desert willow trees, lush vegetation, and sometimes water. This is a great spot for watching wildlife as well.

How to Access

Use the west entrance and drive about 6.5 miles, turning left into the Boy Scout Trail trailhead. Hike on Boy Scout Trail for about 1.2 miles until you come to the Willow Hole trailhead.

Trail Info

- 6.9 miles round-trip
- about 4 hours to hike

Indian Cove

This area is home to our favorite boulders in the park, towering Mojave yuccas, and it has its very own entrance in Twentynine Palms (no park pass is necessary here). While it's actually a campground, there are a few trails off of it such as Indian Cove Nature Trail, access to Boy Scout Trail, and Rattlesnake Canyon. We love coming here to scramble on boulders or park our car, Scout, for a simple picnic.

How to Access

Indian Cove has its own entrance between the north and west entrances. Head east on Route 62 and turn right on Indian Cove Road. Follow this for about three miles into the campground.

Trail Info

INDIAN COVE NATURE TRAIL

- 0.6-mile loop
- about 30 minutes to hike

BOY SCOUT TRAIL

- 8 miles one-way
- around 4–6 hours

Pine City

This is an easy hike with a lot of great flora to see. As the trail progresses, it takes you through some large monzogranite boulders, which creates a cool and moist environment for piñon pines to grow.

How to Access

Use the north entrance and drive about 9.6 miles. Turn right on Desert Queen Mine Road and continue for 1.3 miles. The trailhead is just off the parking area.

Trail Info

- 4.4-mile loop
- about 4 hours to hike

Cholla Garden

This expansive garden full of teddy bear chollas is a magical sight and one of our favorite spots in the park. A simple winding boardwalk leads you through the natural cactus garden, and it particularly glows at sunset. Though this garden looks soft and cuddly, make sure not to get too close or touch the cholla. The spines of a cholla cactus can be incredibly difficult to remove—at the start of the trail there's even a cholla first-aid kit which consists simply of a pair of needle-nose pliers.

How to Access

Use the north entrance and drive about 4.5 miles. Turn left on Pinto Basin Mine Road and continue for 9.8 miles. The trailhead is just off the parking area on the right.

Trail Info

- 0.25-mile loop
- about 20 minutes to walk

Arch Rock Trail at White Tank

Arch Rock Trail is a path attached to the White Tank Campground. It's full of white tank granite, which creates particularly beautiful formations. Following the trail leads to an arch rock and sculpted channels and mazes of smooth white tank granite. This is also a great area of the park for night photography.

Trail Info

- 0.3-mile loop
- about 30 minutes to hike

How to Access

Use the north entrance and drive about 4.5 miles. Turn left on Pinto Basin Mine Road and continue for 2.7 miles. Turn left into the White Tank Campground and follow the signs to the Arch Rock Trail, which is near campsite number nine.

Fortynine Palms Oasis

Throughout most of the park Joshua trees steal the show; however, in this special oasis the desert fan palms take center stage. The trail leads to a natural spring with towering palms that offer much needed shade on a sunny day.

How to Access

Headed east on Route 62 and turn right onto Canyon Road. Follow Canyon Road as it turns slightly to the left and becomes Fortynine Palms Canyon Road. Follow this road until it dead-ends at the trailhead parking lot.

Trail Info

- 3 miles round-trip
- about 2 hours

COWBOY SUMMERS

Back in the 1990s, the previous owners of our Hacienda and Casita bought stock tanks typically used for providing cattle or horses with drinking water and repurposed them as small pools. They lovingly called them "cowboy tubs." Now symbols of summer, these cowboy tubs provide us with a retreat from high desert temperatures of up to 115 degrees Fahrenheit. An afternoon spent in our cowboy tub can give us the shivers on a hot summer day. It's a magical feeling.

Method

FIND YOUR LOCATION To set up a stock tank pool of your own, find a level spot and measure how much open space is available. At the House we have an 8-foot tub, and at the Casita we have a single-person tub that's about 4 feet long and oval. You may need to do some light grading to make a large enough level area for the tank. We chose to place ours directly on the sand, but putting down pavers or stone works great too.

ADD A PUMP Once you have your stock tank in place, you can either add a pump or simply fill it with water. Adding a pump will increase the life span of the pool water by keeping the water moving and preventing mildew from forming. Because water is such a precious resource, we recommend getting a pump in order to conserve water.

You can find a small pool pump at your local pool store for around $100. The pump will need to be plugged in, so plan on either having an electrician add power near the stock tank or a contractor-grade outdoor extension cord handy.

The easiest method to pump water through your cowboy tub will be to simply hang the hose over the side of the pool so it's in the water. Secure it with some weight such as rocks so that it doesn't move.

You'll Need

Stock tank (*Incredibly accessible, stock tanks can be found at most farm supply shops. Though they range in widths, they're usually around two feet tall. While that may not sound very deep, it's plenty to be mostly submerged and fully relaxed.*)

Small pool pump (*Some will come with filters.*)

Metal drill bit and drill

Plumber's putty

Electrician or outdoor contractor-grade extension cord

Chlorine or other pool cleaners of choice

However, the cleanest method is to cut a hole in the side of the tank to connect the pump to. To do this, cut a hole in the back or the least visible area of the tank by using a metal drill bit sized to fit your pump hose. Insert the hose through your new hole, and connect it with a nut. Put a line of plumber's putty around the nut to seal the connection and prevent leakage.

STYLE Once the pool is set up, add plants and rocks to the surrounding area. Allow the exterior of your tub to slowly age as we have, or paint it for a modernized look.

Afternoon

Walking through our garden one afternoon, we were greeted by a tortoise who often strolled by our house (we named her Lady). As we watched her, we saw a bit of movement farther down the path. A baby tortoise, no larger than the palm of our hands tottered through the sand and onto our fence's edge. Like a small seesaw, she rocked back and forth on the bottom of her shell before tumbling off the fence upside down. The urge to help was overridden by intuition not to interfere with nature and to let the young tortoise find her way. Quicker than we expected, she righted herself and continued to explore.

Afternoons represent a shift in the day and a transition to the next. Either static air retains the heat of the midday sun or winds begin to blow if the weather has decided to cool off. In the summer, the heat of midday multiplies, making afternoon the sleepiest time. A break is needed to rest and creatively reset.

In this transition out of midday, it's a time to appreciate slow movements and activities. Take a pause for a repeated and mindless action that will slowly progress.

Working with the elements around us such as the dry air and desert sand, we have enjoyed spending afternoons slowly drying persimmons (*hoshigaki*) and creating paint pigments from sand. The movements of both creations are slow and methodical and lead to the most rewarding results.

CREATING PAINT PIGMENTS WITH SAND

Stella Maria Baer is a painter, desert lover, and previous artist in residence of the Joshua Tree House. For years, she has gathered samples of sand from various deserts in order to make her own paint pigments. In her work she draws out a sense of feeling at home in a place that looks like another world. She connects to her work by painting with pigments born from the landscapes that inspire her most.

For many years she was mixing paints to recreate the colors of the desert, but through experimentation she discovered that she could make pigments not only inspired by the desert, but produced from the landscape itself. We love that Stella uses the sand of our earth to paint the moon and other planets. It feels especially appropriate to see her painting moons with pigments from Joshua Tree when oftentimes living here feels like another planet entirely. Similar to life in the desert, painting in spheres offers Stella both a sense of limitation and liberation.

You'll Need

Trowel

Collection of small recycled jars for gathering sand and for containing your pigments (*You'll need at least one jar per pigment.*)

Sand or dirt

Fine sieve

Mortar and pestle

Gum arabic

While it's one thing to step back and view the desert landscape from afar, it is another thing entirely to bend down on our hands and knees and closely inspect the earth beneath us. As you gather a handful of sand from a winding wash, or from between boulders, you'll notice shifts in color from various elevations and deserts. Each location holds its own stories, and this process of creating pigments with sand is both meditative and enlightening to the vast history of the desert landscape. Before using the recipe below to create your own pigments, we suggest taking a late afternoon walk through the desert with a focus on the sand beneath your feet. Let a handful of sand run between your fingers, and notice the varying textures and colors.

Method

GATHER Take a short hike and start the process by gathering some sand or dirt—a handful or two will be enough to get started. Notice shifts in color, and gather a few variations to experiment with. Always ask permission when gathering on public or private lands.

SIFT THE SAND Shake the sand through a fine sieve into a jar. Discard any rocks, lumps, or debris that may remain in the sieve.

GRIND Grind the sifted sand with a mortar and pestle to further refine the pigments.

ADD WATER Place the ground sand in a jar and add water to fill the small jar halfway, making sure to mix the sand and water together. The heaviest and coarsest particles will sink to the bottom, and the finest particles will remain suspended in the water. Pour the finest particles into another jar, and allow this mixture sit for several hours in the sun or until the water has evaporated.

ADD BINDER Mix the pigment with gum arabic, a traditional binder for watercolor paints. For powdered gum arabic, mix 1 part powder to 2 parts warm water, then dissolve the pigment into the mixture. Add more pigment for a richer color and a smaller amount to create a wash to be mixed with other paints.

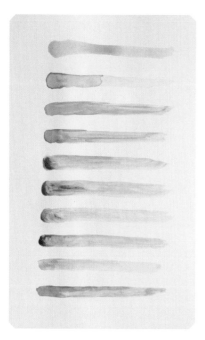

Paint samples made from sand
and cacti by Stella Maria Baer

STORE Once you've created your sand pigments, we recommend storing them in small glass jars. The shelf life of each pigment will vary depending on frequency of use and your climate.

PRACTICE THIS AT HOME Bring your sand pigments, some watercolor paper, a small cup of water, and watercolor brushes outside to observe your environment. There are abstract elements all around us waiting to be painted.

How does your surrounding landscape make you feel? Is it peaceful, or frantic? How do light and shadow enunciate the forms around you? Zoom in on your surroundings, and observe the textures. If you're in the desert, this could be the repeating patterns of cacti spines or the speckled coloring of the sand itself.

Without placing any expectations on the result of your painting—we know this can be difficult—allow yourself to paint freely and playfully. The purpose of this practice is not to have the ultimate piece of work to share with the world, but to allow yourself to let loose. Simply sitting, observing your environment, and painting what you see or feel, make up a meditation of their own.

ENTERTAINING AS
AN EXTENSION OF HOME

◆ ◆ ◆

Entertaining can easily become an overcomplicated additional layer to life, but it doesn't need to be that way. Boxes of holiday decor and dishware stashed away for special occasions are a thing of the past. Curating well-made items that are both beautiful and functional throughout your home means that those pieces are there to help rather than inhibit you as one more thing to store away.

One of our favorite and most used items in our kitchen would be wooden serving boards. We keep a couple of them out on our counter year-round, and not only do they look beautiful stacked along our countertop, they also keep us prepared for any spur-of-the-moment gatherings. These simple boards are a favorite example of entertaining as a natural extension of our daily lifestyle.

As time goes on, the wood boards wear in beautifully, and each mark tells a story of a gathering with friends or family. For Thanksgiving, our friends Thao Nguyen and Anthony Angelicola brought over a beautiful wooden serving board overflowing with various cheeses, nuts, and *hoshigaki*. As owners of our local Joshua Tree furniture design studio, Fire on the Mesa, of course their serving boards were custom made in their shop with an attention to detail and a shared celebration of the imperfection found in natural materials. The thoughtfully created serving boards made of maple and walnut were not only a natural way to add warmth and texture to the table, but they became a conversation piece with the addition of *hoshigaki*.

Hoshigaki are persimmons dried in a slow and traditional Japanese method. The method itself is a reminder to slow down and adds a layer of thoughtfulness particularly appreciated when enjoying the final dried fruits with a gathering of friends.

For weeks before our gathering, Thao and Anthony strung persimmons throughout their home to allow our dry climate to take hold. There's no use in resisting the dryness of the desert, while recipes such as this one thoroughly embrace and utilize it.

With a bit of patience and care, in three to five weeks you will have your very own dried fruits to add to serving boards and offer as a thoughtful addition to dinner parties.

THE ART OF *HOSHIGAKI*

Method

PEEL Peel your persimmons, and be mindful to leave the top stem and cap attached.

ATTACH SCREWS (OPTIONAL) If your persimmon doesn't have a stem, use the screwdriver to attach the screw to the top by slowly rotating a single screw near the center of the leaves. Leave about three-quarters of an inch of the screw visible to attach your cotton string to.

CUT AND TIE STRINGS Cut a 2-foot-long cotton string and attach a persimmon to each end of the string. The string will be draped over your pole, and the weight of the persimmons on either end will hold it in place. Make sure to knot the string onto each persimmon tightly to support the weight of each fruit.

SANITIZE Set your pot of water to boil, and dunk each string of peeled persimmons into the boiling water for about 20 seconds. This helps sanitize your persimmon.

HANG Lay your long pole horizontally (between two surfaces/chairs) and drape your peeled persimmon strands over it, allowing the weight on either side to hold them in place.

DRY Once all of your persimmons are hung, find a cool, dry area away from birds or direct sunlight to hang your pole of persimmons to dry. Eaves of an outdoor porch or inside your home will work perfectly. It's a beautiful presentation reminiscent of fall, so pick a spot where you'll get to enjoy watching the drying process.

MASSAGE Leave the persimmons for three to four days until they have formed a dry skin. Then with clean hands, massage the persimmons gently. Leave them for a few more days and massage again. After a thick skin has formed, each time you massage the fruits, try to gently break up the inside pulp. This helps the sugars form and makes the persimmon sweeter.

You'll Need

24 persimmons (*Ideally these should be on the firmer side and with a stem still attached for stringing. You can make hoshigaki with as many persimmons as you'd like, but we'd suggest a group of two dozen or so to fully enjoy your efforts. Keep in mind that persimmon season is generally from October through mid-January.*)

Peeler

1-inch stainless steel screws and a screwdriver, if your persimmons don't have stems

Cotton string

Small pot filled with water

Long pole for hanging your persimmons (*We used bamboo plant stakes from our local hardware store.*)

Take a moment each day to gently massage your persimmons and enjoy the process.

Repeat the massaging process for three to five weeks. You'll notice your persimmons shrivel as the water within them evaporates. If you prefer a soft texture to your dried fruit, try taking them down in 3–4 weeks, and if you like them fully dried, try leaving them hanging for about 5 weeks.

Keep in mind that the drying time depends on your climate at home. Here in the desert, we are able to work with the dryness of our climate, which speeds up the process.

ENJOY Slice a single persimmon into 4 or 5 pieces and enjoy on a fruit and cheese board, in oatmeal or trail mix, or simply on its own. They also make a simple and thoughtful gift wrapped in parchment paper and leftover cotton string.

PRESERVE Store leftover persimmons in an airtight container.

Fruit and Cheese Board

(suggestions from Fire on the Mesa for a well-balanced fruit & cheese board)

- Large round maple board with a handle for a dinner party
- Small bean-shaped walnut board for everyday use
- Chevre
- Manchego
- Brie
- *Hoshigaki*
- Grapes
- Strawberries
- Currants
- Blackberries
- Figs
- Seeded crackers
- Walnuts or pecans
- Honey
- Fig spread

To care for your wooden serving boards, wash them with warm water and soap after use. Let them dry fully and wipe a bit of mineral oil on them to rehydrate. Mineral oil can be applied every so often, though it's not necessary to apply every time. Any cut marks can be sanded with very fine sandpaper.

Sunset

Just after sunset we looked up to see movement in the boulders. We pulled out a flashlight and binoculars and saw an animal that looked to be half the size of one of the smaller boulders. Our eyes still adjusting to the darkness, we wondered if the animal before us could be a bighorn sheep or coyote. Just then its head rotated, and a great horned owl took off—its wings covering the darkening sky.

Sunset is a reminder to get outside and enjoy the moment. Though each night's sky varies, this sentiment remains the same. The glowing desert landscape makes us feel as if we live in a dream, and it surfaces a curiosity in the details around us. Knowing that the light will soon fade, we take it all in while we can. Contradiction surrounds us—while one side of the sky paints vivid colors of reds and oranges in the clouds, the reverse side creates a perfect gradient of purples and pinks.

Desert wildlife such as coyotes, roadrunners, and jackrabbits run through the scene, taking advantage of the day's last bits of light. We pay attention to which animals we see and name the regulars. These animals are our new neighbors, teaching us lessons as we go.

No matter the season, a cocktail at sunset is a favorite way to entertain both ourselves and friends. You'll find our favorite cocktail in this section—an ode to the simplicity of homestead life and the showmanship of the sun as it sets.

ANIMAL SYMBOLS

❖❖❖

As the sun begins to set, a break in the day is welcomed as a reward for the hard work that came before it. The wildlife around us begins to shuffle, some ready to end their day, while other nocturnal creatures are ready to begin. Since our move to Joshua Tree, we've taken cues from the varying wildlife that has crossed our path—we've found patterns in the frequency of particular animal appearances in our lives to align with our own personal triumphs and struggles. The desert has given us time and space to pay attention to the wildlife around us as meaningful symbols. We've found ourselves not only noticing *which* animals we see, but *when* we see them and what's occurring in our own lives at that moment.

We've particularly been inspired to pay attention to these symbols with the influence of our desert neighbor Caris Reid, who is a painter, tarot reader, and Reiki master. Caris is highly intuitive and has inspired us to closely observe our environment and notice more than just the details of our experiences, but also the symbolism that those experiences hold. The stories she's shared with us of her life here in Joshua Tree have pushed us to consider the symbols around us. Often, these symbols are the wildlife native to the desert that scurry by or gracefully appear before us in unsuspecting but essential moments.

"During the heat of the summer I was sitting on my front porch, meditating. It had been a few weeks since I'd been in the studio. Events in my personal life were demanding a lot of my attention, and I had been neglecting my work. I sat, quietly, focused inward, eyes closed. And when I opened my eyes and scanned the horizon, there was a giant snake stretched across the door of my studio. The message couldn't have been clearer. I was being called to reawaken my dormant kundalini energy, that fire of creativity, and reenter my studio—which I did, later that same day."

—Caris Reid, *painter*

Caris, are there any particular experiences in Joshua Tree with an animal that stand out to you, aside from the snake experience?

There was a day this summer in August, during monsoon season, when the power went out. It was hot. In the 100s. With the power out, so was the cooling air. I was on deadline for a show, so sitting and sweating, working on a painting. And because there was no electricity, I couldn't listen to music, so was sitting in silence. I had been working, quietly, all day long, in the heat, when a loud thud hit the window. Startled, I got up, and peered outside, and saw a beautiful hawk sitting there. I grabbed my camera and stepped outside to snap a photo of this majestic creature. After it flew away, I came back inside to find the power had turned back on. My whole body got goose bumps. It was incredibly powerful.

What are some other meaningful symbols you bring into your painting practice?

Part of the power of symbols is their ability to communicate information to our subconscious without our conscious mind getting in the way. There is a deep wisdom within all of us that just *knows* without having been told. I gravitate toward the use of symbolism in my work, because I'm interested in activating a more intuitive and primal space within the viewer. I incorporate symbols that are common, like the peace sign, or that have history and meaning, like a rune.

New York and Joshua Tree are both full of life in very different ways. Has this contrast of environment made its way into your work since your move to the desert?

They really are, but both places have an intensity to them, which I enjoy. The difference has made an impact on my schedule and rituals. In New York I used to burn the candle on both ends, I was working hard, staying out late, and digesting as much culture as possible. In Joshua Tree, I'm in bed most nights by 9 p.m. I wake up with the sun, my days are slow, disciplined. and solitary. I'm sure it's reflected in the work, but I can't pinpoint it yet.

How has being a Reiki master and tarot reader related to your practice as a painter?

My approach to painting is incredibly intuitive, and that sensibility has such a natural connection to tarot and Reiki. Reiki is a healing technique I use on a daily basis, and I always start every painting by laying a hand on its surface and sending it Reiki light. It's a small and quiet ritual, but one that is important to me and signifies the start of the process. Tarot has a less direct connection to the paintings, but because of my interest in symbolism and archetypes, I have painted several paintings inspired by the tarot, such as *The High Priestess* and *The Empress*.

As you read through the animal symbols that follow, remember that these symbols are places to begin surfacing themes or concepts that you may already intuitively know are apparent in your life. A recent animal sighting either physically or in your dreams may become more meaningful with the understanding of these symbols. But if not, that's okay too. No matter the outcome, our hope is that you will become more aware of your environment and enjoy the creatures that do appear along your path.

Coyote

The coyote is the trickster of the desert, the playful hunter, the shape-shifter. When the coyote appears before you, it's important to note: Who are you with? What are you saying? What are you thinking? Because of the mercurial nature of the coyote, the symbolism isn't fixed. This is a part of the medicine. The coyote invites us to question if things are as they seem—often in the presence of the coyote, the answer is no.

Sometimes the coyote appears as a word of warning, a note to be cautious. In other moments, it's an invitation to bring in more play into your life. As you watch the coyote move along the desert, you'll notice a lightness to the movement, almost a skip. Are you needing to invite levity into your life?

Roadrunner

The message of the roadrunner is much like the movement of this swift bird: instant, direct, and clear. When the roadrunner appears before you, it's a call for action, movement, travel, and adrenaline. It's a sign of healing or the completion of a transformation or goal, and offers the encouragement to move forward with confidence.

The roadrunner appeared to us consistently throughout several months as we tirelessly created one of our largest and most collaborative projects to date. Every time we saw this beautiful bird sprint by, we knew our forward motion was leading to something good.

Snake

The snake is simultaneously one of the most feared and mystical creatures of the desert. Through the winter months they rest in hibernation, readying to hunt in the spring. The wisdom of the snake is like that of the moon: to operate in cycles. When the snake appears, it's time to reconnect to your body, your senses, as well as your instinct to move and create. Snakes feel the vibrations of the earth and make their movements accordingly.

Allow the snake to guide you in a similar manner to move forward in connection with your sexuality, creativity, and spirituality. The snake is also a powerful symbol of rebirth. When a snake sheds its skin, it sheds a layer completely. When the snake appears, it's time to connect to your body as well as your instincts. This could be a sign that a personal transformation is unfolding. Caris's story of the snake stretched in front of her studio after a period of neglecting her practice is a beautiful example of the snake's symbology.

Desert Quail

When the quail appears, *quails* appear—it's rare to see a single quail roaming about. These birds move in flocks, and that's precisely the message that they bring. The quail represents community and family. What's your relationship to your community? Have you been isolated? The quail invites you to reconnect with those around you.

Lizard

The lizard has the ability to shed its tail for the purpose of survival, leaving a part of itself behind with its predator. The lizard is a symbol of regeneration, healing, and self-love. It serves as a reminder to let go of objects or ways of life that are no longer serving us and of our power to create change and forward motion.

During our first year of living in Joshua Tree, a chuckwalla (a large lizard) made the spot right outside of our bathroom window his home. We would see him every day, a reminder of the lifestyle we had just left in San Francisco that was no longer serving us.

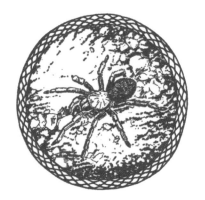

Tarantula

Spotting this unhurried and gentle creature is a sign to slow down and trust that everything will be okay. It's a reminder not to worry about the future and to be patient. Trust that whatever you've been working on will come to fruition, but it's time to step back and let things take hold on their own. Finding balance is key to a stable foundation.

We spotted a tarantula with friends that we had recently decided to work with on a new design project. The project had lots of potential for worry, but this sighting was a reminder that often events unfold on their own. We knew it was time to trust that this project would unfold as we hoped it would with a balance of work and rest.

Bee

Though sometimes seen alone, where there is one bee, there are usually others close by. They are hardworking creatures, who act together as a team. When the bee appears, it may be asking you to consider your relationship to your community and to productivity. Are you working too hard? Or not enough? Bees are pollinators, which symbolically speak to one's ability to share and spread inspiration. The work they do is always to strengthen and better their community, and symbolically they ask you how you can do the same.

Hummingbird

The hummingbird is a tiny creature, but one that moves with great speed. The hummingbird is symbolic of movement, lightness, and joy. When the hummingbird appears, it can be a sign to enjoy the nectars of life and return to the things that feed your spirit. It can also be a sign that it's time to move swiftly.

Crow

The crow, like all birds, is a messenger between the physical and spiritual worlds. It is associated with magic, creation, and nocturnal energy. There is a mischievous and sometimes chaotic energy with the crow, but when harnessed correctly, that is a catalyst for great creative energy.

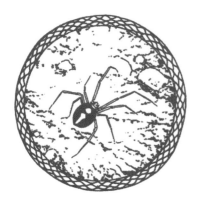

Black Widow

The black widow is connected to creation and destruction. She is equally capable of both. She weaves her web with great intricacy and care and is therefore associated with heightened creativity. Despite her delicate and fragile frame, she is known for her deadly bite and sexual cannibalism. Because of this she is also symbolic of a darker feminine energy.

Mourning Dove

Mourning doves are almost always seen in pairs. They are monogamous birds who are symbolic of lasting partnership. These graceful creatures were given their name because of the sad sound to their call. Like all doves, they are associated with peace and hope.

Bighorn Sheep

Spotting a bighorn sheep is a sign of new beginnings and confidence on the path ahead. If you're lucky enough to have a bighorn sheep cross your path, you'll see a strong and confident creature before you. It's a sign to use that optimistic energy in your own life and a reminder not to question our own abilities. It's time to take a leap.

We spotted one of these beautiful creatures in Joshua Tree National Park just before the new year. The timing couldn't have been more appropriate, as we were reminded to continue on our path with confidence. The way he stood so self-assured before us, climbing straight up boulders without a second thought, has stuck with us. Now, every time we question our abilities, we're reminded of this incredible creature.

Tortoise

Tortoises take their time to stop and rest often. Meditative creatures, they represent creativity, contentment, and peace. If the tortoise appears before you, it may be a reminder to take a break from the busyness of life and find serenity. It's often said that life is short, but the tortoise reminds us that life is long. There's always time to be made for days full of creativity and peace.

Our first year living in Joshua Tree, a sweet desert tortoise stopped by our screen door every day and simply sat there until we would come outside. We would take a moment to sit with the tortoise, cut up a cactus fruit for her, and then she would be on her way. We like to think she was teaching us to slow down as we transitioned into our new life in the desert.

Scorpion

Spotting a scorpion reminds us to consider toxicity in our lives. Are there relationships or situations best removed from your life? A scorpion stings for self-preservation, which presents an opportunity to break free. Remove the clutter from your life both physically and mentally to discover a personal rebirth.

Jackrabbit

Rabbits are fertile creatures and represent fertility either physically or creatively.

If you're considering having children, the appearance of a jackrabbit could be a sign that you are ready. It could also be a sign of fertility in creative projects or ideas. Rabbits are quick to run and can be a symbol of fear or anxiety as well. A jackrabbit in your path can be a sign to move past irrational fears and continue forward.

Hawk

The hawk's vision is sharp and clear. A powerful bird messenger, it circles the sky, quietly assessing the landscape and watching for movement and signs of prey. As a masterful hunter, the hawk's motions are precise and impactful. Like all birds, the hawk is a connector between the physical world and the spiritual world. The hawk brings the medicine of discernment and seeing situations with both a spiritual and logical sense. When the hawk appears, it's time to see your life from a higher vantage point. How is this moment connected to your larger journey and life purpose? Are you overly focused on the minutiae? The hawk asks you to see the larger picture and to take confident action from that perspective.

HONORING SIMPLICITY

◆ ◆ ◆

On a drive through Joshua Tree, small abandoned homesteads scatter the landscape. We love to imagine what kind of stories those cabins hold about the bold personalities who built them in search of a simple life.

In 1938, the Small Tract Act was passed, incentivizing homesteaders to prove up the land by building a small structure (at least twelve by six feet) in order to be deeded a five-acre tract. It was a chance to live with few possessions and an open horizon. The harsh climate of the desert proved too tough for many in the end, but these scattered homesteads remind us of why we're here: to live out a simple dream where sunsets are never missed and animals are our neighbors—to live wild.

Some nights as the sun begins to lower, we head outside to watch it with a cocktail in hand. You'll find our favorite recipe below, named in honor of simplicity.

THE HOMESTEADER COCKTAIL

Method

STIR Pour 1 part mezcal and 2 parts tonic into your lowball glass, and stir to combine.

PALO SANTO Use your peeler to shave a thin curl of orange peel. Light a stick of palo santo and hold the smoke under the peel for 10–20 seconds. Twist the orange peel above the glass and place into the drink.

GARNISH If you have rosemary in your garden, try adding a small sprig to the top of your glass for a sensory experience.

You'll Need

1 ounce mezcal

2 ounce tonic

Orange peel

Sprig of rosemary

Lowball cocktail glass

Stick of palo santo

Matches

Evening

One summer night during the Perseid meteor shower, we sat out under the stars. Do you know the sensation when the air is so still and warm that you can't feel the difference between your own body and the air around you? That was that night. We looked up in awe to meteors whizzing by and realized that desert summers will always have our hearts.

The evening's loss of sunlight means that temperatures cool just as quickly as our minds and bodies tire. We often joke that desert midnight runs a little early here, setting in at around nine p.m.

Desert evenings bring with them two distinct choices: to settle in for the night or to head outside and extend desert midnight a little longer. A hot bath with chaparral and petrified wood allows us to end the day by soaking in the desert of our dreams, while stargazing and nighttime photography provide an entirely new perspective on the desert landscape we so love.

DESERT BATHING
WITH CHAPARRAL

❖ ❖ ❖

We met Sophia Rose, an herbalist, during an event she hosted here in Joshua Tree. She took us on a plant walk through the desert and reminded us of the relationships we have with plants around us. Instinctually, we often take from nature, but her first impulse was to give. As we stopped at a beavertail cactus, she offered up some of her water to the thirsty plant. We recommend that as you prepare the following bath recipe created by Sophia, you also consider offering something back to the desert in exchange for a clipping of chaparral.

Chaparral
GOBERNADORA, CREOSOTE

This potent medicinal shrub characterizes the landscape of Southern California. Its deep green expanse is in stark contrast to the endless sky and stretches like the ocean as far as the eye can see. As you drive down the desolate highways and country back roads, it is the ancient and thrumming presence of chaparral that calls forth the precious solitude and stark beauty offered only by the desert. Its resinous leaves hold the scent and memory of the soaking rains of many thousands of seasons past. Submerged in a hot bath along with a couple of its potent branches, you'll find yourself steeped in the desert of your dreams and taken to a place of deep awakening, heightened psychic awareness, and unexpected resilience.

A profound antiseptic, chaparral is an indispensable desert ally. It helps to prevent infections in wounds, soothes bites and stings, as well as bringing sweet relief to eczema, psoriasis, and fungal infections of both the skin and the scalp. It even helps

Photo by David Benhaim

to soothe acne, boils, and other eruptive skin conditions. It is one of our favorite plants to soak alongside after a day spent in the sun. The unequaled antioxidant properties of this ancient desert plant help to repair free radical damage, keeping skin healthy, glowing, and resilient even in the harshest of climates. We recommend adding a couple of small branches to a hot bath, along with a piece of petrified wood for a grounding and distinctive therapeutic experience. Do note, though, that the scent of chaparral is quite strong and may be a bit too intense for many. We are desert folks at heart, however, and love it without apology or qualification.

CHAPARRAL BATH

Method

GATHER Gather a few small chaparral branches using garden clippers.

FILL TUB Place the boughs and some petrified wood (known for its grounding and calming energies) in the bath, and fill the tub with hot water. If you don't have access to fresh chaparral, add a couple of dropperfuls of chaparral oil to your hot bath.

SOAK Soak in the magic of the Mojave...

NEW MOON
PHOTOGRAPHY GUIDE

◆ ◆ ◆

On the new moon, the earth, moon, and sun align, making us unaware of the moon's presence in the sky. Without the moon's visual presence and glow, other celestial bodies typically hidden now shine brighter. Our chances of seeing the sky clearly are heightened on this day, making it a day of clarity and new beginnings. Creatively it's the perfect time to set intentions for a new cycle of dreams and goals and ways of manifesting them.

Looking up to the sky on this night, we're in awe of the constellations and shooting stars blazing across the firmament. Most nights, we simply lay back and stare in an attempt to take it all in. On occasion we're filled with the desire to capture the beauty and power of this night—and though it's impossible to pin down the incredible presence of the stars—we attempt to.

Photo by David Benhaim

NIGHTTIME PHOTOGRAPHY IN PRACTICE

The Basics

SHUTTER SPEED Shutter speed is measured in seconds or parts of a second. The Canon 5D Mark III that we use has a shutter speed range of 1/8000th of a second to 30 seconds, meaning that the shutter on our camera can stay open for up to 30 seconds in order to let enough light in to capture the scene. A fast shutter speed is used to capture movement or a subject in daylight. While shooting the night sky, you'll want a long exposure with a shutter speed of around 20–30 seconds.

APERTURE The aperture refers to the size of the hole that lets light into the camera, controlled by the f-stop. When the shutter is open, adjusting the f-stop to have a larger lens opening increases the exposure. Depth of field is also controlled with the f-stop: an f-stop of f/22 puts the whole scene before you in focus. However, if you'd like to have something in the foreground in focus and everything in the distance out of focus, set your f-stop to around f/2.8 (or lower if your lens allows) to accomplish a shallow depth of field. For nighttime photography, use the lowest f-stop. In our case, f/2.8 works great and will get as much light to the sensors as possible.

ISO ISO is the abbreviated name of the International Organization for Standardization and indicates the industry standard for measuring light sensitivity. Typical ISOs range from 100 to 6400. The lower the ISO, the less sensitive the camera is to light. Higher numbers make the camera more sensitive to light, but can also make your image appear grainy and quickly degrade image quality.

COMPOSITION Stepping out in the darkness to take a photo can feel like photographing blind. In order to find a composition you like, you may have to take a few test shots to see what's in your frame.

Method

Before heading outside to capture the night sky, take a deep breath and remind yourself that the beauty of nature is its unpredictability. Understand that some nights may bring clouds, light pollution, or wind that can make the stars difficult to photograph. That's absolutely okay—a static sky would lose its allure.

ADJUST APERTURE Turn your aperture down as low as your lens allows. On the lens we use that's f/2.8, but this can vary and could be something like f/4. While that doesn't seem like a big difference between the 2 apertures, the f/2.8 will allow much more light in.

SET ISO Set your camera to 3200 ISO with a 30-second shutter speed with the lowest f-stop possible, and take a test shot. In order to avoid a grainy photo, our friend and photographer David Benhaim recommends refraining from taking a shot with an ISO over 3200. If using a lower ISO, you may need to increase your shutter speed by changing your camera setting to "bulb" and using a remote shutter device to keep the shutter open for longer than the camera settings allow for.

CHANGE SHUTTER SPEED Change the shutter speed to around 30 seconds, and take a test shot. If you want to use a lower ISO setting, you can buy an attachment for your camera to manually keep the shutter open for a set amount of time.

FOCUS Shine a strong flashlight onto the subject in the foreground (for example, a Joshua tree) to focus the lens. Use a self-timer of 2 seconds on your camera in order to remove any camera shake from pressing the trigger, or use a remote trigger to take the photo.

CAPTURE THE SKY Based off these initial settings, adjust the aperture, shutter speed, and ISO for your specific environment. Enjoy a beautiful evening under the stars, and snap a photo to capture the moment.

You'll Need

DSLR or mirrorless camera (*We use a Canon 5D Mark III, but most DSLRs or mirrorless cameras by Canon, Sony, Nikon, Fuji, and Leica will work great.*)

Lens with a large aperture such as 1.8 or 2.8 (*We use a wide-angle zoom 16–35mm f/2.8L lens, though Prime lenses are ideal for the sharpest image.*)

Tripod (*We use a Manfrotto Befree travel tripod.*)

Military-grade LED flashlight (*We use this to shine on foreground subjects such as Joshua trees while focusing the shot.*)

Remote trigger (*optional, but can be used to reduce camera shake*)

Snack, warm beverage, layers, and chair if you plan on being out for a while (*optional*)

Sky Village Swap Meet

Resource Guide

JOSHUA TREE SHOPS

Acme 5
A great shop for furniture and home decor in Yucca Valley.
@shopacme5lifestyle
www.acme5lifestyle.com

All Roads Studio
Janelle Pietrzak and Robert Dougherty's studio and store in Yucca Valley. Stop by to see Janelle's weavings and Robert's metalwork.
@all_roads_studio
www.allroadsdesign.com

The End
Magical curated vintage and designer clothing shop in Yucca Valley.
@theendyuccavalley
theendyuccavalley.com

Hoof & The Horn
Clothing and some home accessories in Yucca Valley.
@hoofandthehorn
www.hoofandthehorn.com

Industry of All Nations
Undyed garment shop in Joshua Tree.
@industryofallnations
industryofallnations.com

Shop on the Mesa

Joshua Tree Rock Shop

A crystal and rock shop, every desert needs one.

@joshuatreerockshop

joshuatreerock-shop.com

Mercado Mojave

A market on Saturdays in the high desert.

@mercadomojave

mojavedesertmarkets.com

The Mincing Mockingbird

Books and stationery etc.

@mincingmockingbird

mincingmockingbird.com

Mojave Flea Trading Post

A marketplace of makers & merchants in Yucca Valley.

@mojaveflea.yuccavalley

shoptradingpost.com

MoonWind Trading Co

A boutique store in Yucca Valley with clothing and accessories.

@moonwindtradingco

moonwindtradingco.com

Soukie Modern

A great place to source Moroccan Rugs in Palm Springs.

@soukiemodern

soukiemodern.com

Sun of The Desert

A General Store in the High Desert.

@sunofthedesert_

sunofthedesert.com

The Station

Souvenir shop in Joshua Tree.

@thestationjoshuatree

www.thestationjoshuatreehouse.com

Wine & Rock Shop

A great place for natural wines and other gifts.

@wineandrockshop

wineandrockshop.com

Xēba Botánica

A shop with natural skincare in Pioneertown.

@xebabotanica

xebabotanica.com

JOSHUA TREE FOOD

Boo's Organic Oven

A bakery in Joshua Tree with delicious baked goods and bread.

@boosorganicoven

The Copper Room

A bar and restaurant along the airport runway in Yucca Valley.

Country Kitchen

A great spot to get a classic American breakfast and Cambodian food.

@jtcountrykitchen

Crossroads

Great for any meal in downtown Joshua Tree.

crossroadscafejtree.com

Desierto Alto

A bodega in Yucca Valley with wine, spirits and snacks.

@desierto_alto

desiertoalto.com

The Dez Fine Foods

Takeaway food and coffee in downtown Joshua Tree.

@dezfinefood

dezfinefood.com

Frontier Cafe

A coffee shop with Wi-Fi located in Yucca Valley. We often go there to work on our laptops and get coffee or lunch.

@cafefrontier

www.cafefrontier.com

Holistic Ranch

A natural grocer and general goods in Yucca Valley.

@holisticranch

holisticranch.com

Joshua Tree Brewery

Locally brewed beer in Joshua Tree.

@joshuatreebrewery

joshuatreebrewery.com

Joshua Tree Coffee Co.

Coffee shop in Joshua Tree (*get their Nitro!*).

@joshuatreecoffeecompany

jtcoffeeco.com

Joshua Tree Farmers Market

We love coming here on Saturday to pick up fresh local fruit and vegetables from the surrounding areas.

www.joshuatreefarmersmarket.com

Joshua Tree Saloon

A great spot downtown to grab a drink or have some western fare.

@joshua_tree_saloon

www.joshuatreesaloon.com

Kasa Carniceria y Taqueria

This is where we go for a lunchtime taco or to pick up ingredients for our homemade salsa.

56089 Twentynine Palms Highway, Yucca Valley, CA 92284

Kitchen in the Desert

A Caribbean & new American restaurant in 29 Palms with great outdoor seating.

@kitcheninthedesert29

La Copine

Our favorite food in the high desert. This Flamingo Heights restaurant switches its offerings seasonally.

@lacopinekitchen

www.lacopinekitchen.com

Natural Sisters

A healthy food option in downtown Joshua Tree. They have great smoothies and vegetarian options.

@thenaturalsisterscafe

www.naturalsisterscafe.com

Out There Bar

A fun bar in 29 Palms.

@outtherebar

Pappy & Harriets

A must-see in the high desert. They often have a concert going on, and this is a great spot for a drink or barbecue.

@pappyandharriets

www.pappyandharriets.com

Pie for the People

Good pizza in Yucca Valley.

@pieforthepeople

pieforthepeoplepizzadicirco.com

Noah Purifoy Outdoor Museum

Red Dog Saloon

Great cocktails and tacos in Pioneertown.

@reddogpioneertown

reddogpioneertown.com

Royal Siam Thai

Thai food in downtown Joshua Tree.

61599 Twentynine Palms Highway,
Joshua Tree, CA 92252

Sam's Indian

Great Indian food in Joshua Tree with lots of vegetarian options. They also have Indian pizza.

@samsindianfood

www.samsindianfood.com

29 Palms Inn

A nice place to get dinner or a drink near the Oasis of Mara.

@29palmsinn

JOSHUA TREE MEDITATION AND MINDFULNESS

Cedar and Sage Wellness Studio

A yoga studio in Yucca Valley.

@cedarandsagewellnesstudio

Institute of Mental Physics

Walking meditation at the rock mineral labyrinth, as well as mindful events such as Shakti Fest and Bhakti Fest.

www.jtrcc.org

The Integratron

Built by ufologist and contactee George Van Tassel to rejuvenate the human body and time travel, it now provides sound baths in the perfectly acoustic dome. Book early to make sure to get a reservation.

@theintegratron

integratron.com

JOSHUA TREE EXPERIENCES

Crochet Museum

A cute museum in downtown Joshua Tree full of crocheted animals and other objects.

www.sharielf.com/museum.html

Noah Purifoy Outdoor Museum

An outdoor desert art museum of assembled materials by the late artist Noah Purifoy.

@noahpurifoyfoundation

www.noahpurifoy.com

Taylor Junction

They have a nice back yard for shows and often host art gallery openings.

@taylorjunctionjtree

VINTAGE HOME GOODS & ESTATE SALES

Alameda Flea Market

When we lived in San Francisco, we would go to this flea market every month. First Sunday of every month.

www.alamedapointantiquesfaire.com

The Estate Sale Co

A great place to find mid-century furniture from estates and hotels in Palm Springs.

www.theestatesaleco.com

Long Beach Antique Market

Third Sunday of every month.

@longbeachantiquemarket

www.longbeachantiquemarket.com

Pioneer Crossing

One of our favorite places to search for vintage goods in the high desert.

www.pioneercrossingantiques.com

Rosebowl Flea Market

Second Sunday of every month.

@rosebowl_fleamarket

www.rgcshows.com

Route 62

A great spot to find vintage furniture in Yucca Valley.

www.rt62vintagemarketplace.com

Sky Village Swap Meet

Every Saturday and Sunday. It's one of our favorite weekend activities to look through vintage books, records, and find random treasures.

@skyvillagemarketplace

www.skyvillageswapmeet.com

LOCAL CACTUS NURSERIES

Cactus Mart

The dig your own cactus sign is a landmark of Morongo Valley.

@cactus_mart

www.cactusmart.com

Cactus Store

A cactus shop in Los Angeles with a nice curated selection of cacti in simple terra-cotta planters.

@hotcactus_la

hotcactus.la

Mariscal Cactus Nursery

In Desert Hot Springs, this nursery is a jungle of euphorbias and cacti. You can find almost any type of cactus here.

@mariscalcactusnursery

mariscalcactussucculents.com

Moorten Botanical Garden

A beautiful cactus garden and shop in Palm Springs with plants from deserts all over the world.

@moortenbotanicalgarden

moortenbotanicalgarden.com

SUPPORT THE DESERT

Joshua Tree National Park Association

The organization that directly supports Joshua Tree National Park.

www.joshuatree.org

Mojave Desert Land Trust

The MDLT protects the Mojave Desert ecosystem and its scenic and cultural values.

@mojavedesertlandtrust

www.mdlt.org

ARTISTS INSPIRED BY THE DESERT

Stella Maria Baer

@stellamariabaer

www.stellamariabaer.com

Brian Bosworth

@bkbceramics

bkbceramics.com

Angel Chen

@angelchenworld

www.angel-chen.com

Heather Day

@heatherdayart

www.heatherdayart.com

Harrison Fraley

@harrisonfraley

Lindsay Hollinger

@lindsayhollinger

www.casajoshuatree.com

Emily Katz—Modern Macrame

@modernmacrame

modernmacrame.com

Julia Kostreva

@juliakostreva

studio.juliakostreva.com

Tim Melideo

@timmelideo

timmelideo.com

Jen Mussari

@jenmussari

jenmussari.com

Thao Nguyen

@thao_nguyen__

shoponthemesa.com

Janelle Pietrzak

@janelle_pietrzak

www.allroadsdesign.com

Orianna Reardon

@oriannaa

Caris Reid

@carisr

www.carisreid.com

Ryan Schneider

@ryan_schneider_

ryanschneiderart.com

Meghan Shimek

@meghanshimek

meghanshimek.com

Kyle Simon

@kylecanal

www.kylesimonart.com

Kathrin Smirke

@bandsofcolor

www.bandsofcolor.com

Lily Stockman

@lilystockman

www.lilystockman.com

Wilder California

@wildercalifornia

www.wildercalifornia.com

Aleksandra Zee

@aleksandrazee

www.aleksandrazee.com

Andrea Zittel

@andreazittel

zittel.org

NATURAL BEAUTY AND WELLNESS

Tienlyn Jacobson

Writes about wellness and beauty as well as places to explore in Joshua Tree and Palm Springs.

@thoughtfulmisfit

www.thoughtfulmisfit.com

Juniper Ridge

Native plant aromatics.

@juniperridge

juniperridge.com

La Abeja Herbs

Plant medicine and apothecary goods by Sophia Rose.

@laabejaherbs

www.gardenparty.love

laabejaherbs.com

PHOTOGRAPHY

Canon

We use the Canon 5D Mark III, but they recently came out with the Mark IV.

@canonusa

www.usa.canon.com

Fuji

We use the Fuji x100T which is a great travel camera.

@fujifilm_northamerica

www.fujifilmamericas.com

OUTDOORS

Shelter Co.

Luxury tents that can be rented for events or purchased.

@shelterco

shelter-co.com

HOME ACCESSORIES

Aelfie

@aelfie_

aelfie.com

Blacksaw

@blacksaw.co

blacksaw.co

Café Appliances

@cafeappliances

cafeappliances.com

Delta

@deltafaucet

www.deltafaucet.com

EastFork Pottery
@eastforkpottery
eastforkpottery.com

eBay
@ebay
www.ebay.com

Etsy
@etsy
www.etsy.com

Ferm Living
@fermliving
www.fermliving.com

Fireclay Tile
@fireclaytile
www.fireclaytile.com

Floyd
@floyddetroit
www.floyddetroit.com

Framebridge
@framebridge
www.framebridge.com

General Store
@generalstore
shop-generalstore.com

Ikea
@ikea
www.ikea.com

Kohler
@kohlerco
www.kohler.com

Lawson Fenning
@lawsonfenning
lawsonfenning.com

Parachute Home
@parachutehome
www.parachutehome.com

Pop and Scott
@popandscott
www.popandscott.com

Sackcloth & Ashes
@sackclothxashes
sackclothxashes.com

Smeg
@smegusa
www.smegusa.com

Tribe & True
@tribeandtrue
www.tribeandtrue.com

Wanderluxe Jewelry & Home
@wanderluxejewelry
www.wanderluxedesign.com

Year & Day
@yearandday
yearandday.com

LIGHTING AND ELECTRICAL

Badia Design
@badiadesign
www.badiadesign.com

Cedar and Moss
@cedarandmoss
www.cedarandmoss.com

House of Antique Hardware
@houseofantiquehardware.com
www.houseofantiquehardware.com

Pepe and Carols
@pepeandcarols
www.pepeandcarols.com

Schoolhouse Electric
@schoolhouse
www.schoolhouse.com

Selamat
@selamatdesigns
www.selamatdesigns.com

FURNITURE

Anthropologie
@anthropologie
www.anthropologie.com

Article
@article
www.article.com

Barnaby Lane
@barnabylane
www.barnabylaneusa.com

Casper
@casper
casper.com

CB2
@cb2
www.cb2.com

Chairish
@chairishco
www.chairish.com

Fire on the Mesa
@fire_onthe_mesa
fireonthemesa.com

Katie Gong
@katie.gong
www.katiegongdesign.com

Modernica
@modernica
modernica.net

Moodadventures
@moodadventures
www.moodadventures.nl

Rad Weld Customs
@radweldcustoms
www.radweldcustoms.net

Rejuvenation
@rejuvenation
www.rejuvenation.com

Serena & Lily
@serenaandlily
www.serenaandlily.com

Urban Outfitters

@urbanoutfitters

www.urbanoutfitters.com

West Elm

@westelm

www.westelm.com

World Market

@worldmarket

www.worldmarket.com

RUGS AND TEXTILES

Apprvl

@apprvl

www.apprvlnyc.com

Blacksaw

@blacksaw.co

blacksaw.co

Blockshop Textiles

@blockshoptextiles

www.blockshoptextiles.com

East Perry

@eastperry

www.eastperry.com

Lasso Abode

@lasso.abode

www.lassoabode.com

Linen Shed

@linenshed

linenshed.com

Loom + Kiln

@loomandkiln

loomandkiln.com/rugs

Mercado Collective

@mercado.collective

www.mercadocollectivestyle.com

Pampa

@wearepampa

pampa.com.au

Sackcloth & Ashes

@sackclothxashes

sackclothandashes.com

Soukie Modern

@soukiemodern

www.soukiemodern.com

Tribe & True

@tribeandtrue

www.tribetrue.com

Woven Abode

@wovenabode

wovenabode.com

HOME TECHNOLOGY

Amazon

@amazon

www.amazon.com

Apple

@apple

www.apple.com

August Home

@augusthomeinc

august.com

Nest

@nest

nest.com

Philips Hue

@philipshue

www.usa.philips.com

Ring

@ring

ring.com

Schlage

schlage.com

DESERT WEAR

Blundstone

@blundstone

www.blundstone.com

Brookes Boswell

@brookesboswell

www.shopboswel.us

Everlane

@everlane

www.everlane.com

Freda Salvador

@fredasalvador

www.fredasalvador.com

Levi's

@levis

levis.com

Madewell

@madewell

www.madewell.com

Mohinders

@mohindersshoes

www.mohinders.com

West Perro

@westperro

www.westperro.com

FOOD AND GROCERY

DRAM Apothecary

@DramApothecary

dramapothecary.com

Eco Bags

@ecobags_usa

www.ecobags.com

Shreebs Coffee

@shreebscoffee

www.shreebscoffee.com

INSPIRATION SOURCES

Apartment Therapy

@apartmenttherapy

www.apartmenttherapy.com

Architectural Digest

@archdigest

www.architecturaldigest.com

Domino

@dominomag

domino.com

Rue Mag

@ruemagazine

ruemag.com

Photo by Tim Melideo

 # About Us

We are Sara and Rich Combs, high school sweethearts and creators of the Joshua Tree House. We currently live with our two cats in the Mojave Desert of Joshua Tree, California, designing experiences both physical and digital.

At the end of 2013, we both left our full-time jobs as UI/UX designers to pursue running our own design studio. After living and working on the road for a year, we searched for a place to call home. We have now spent the last few years in Joshua Tree, developing an eye for interior design, photography, and lifestyle design while experiencing the breathtaking backdrop of the high desert. Through our curated brand—the Joshua Tree House—we're able to share our passion for creating mindful, memorable experiences.

Starting with the renovation of one very special 1949 hacienda, we shared our process on social media and eventually put our house up for rent on Airbnb to share with others. We were able to connect with those interested in a slow and deliberate desert lifestyle, with an appreciation for small details that celebrate everyday experiences.

OUR STORY

✦ ✦ ✦

It all began with a month long cross-country road trip. We got in a routine of driving a few hours each morning and spending the rest of the day hiking a national park along the route. It was our first time to Joshua Tree, and it felt different than all the rest—something about this place pulled us in and stayed in our thoughts. Exactly one year later, we found ourselves looking to buy a home in Joshua Tree. As soon as we stepped foot onto the property of the Joshua Tree House, we knew it was special and the perfect place to share with others who needed to reflect, reset, and create.

After sharing this place with others, we found it increasingly difficult to leave the desert and head back to the city ourselves. We eventually made the move to the Mojave Desert full-time, a place that at first seems so barren but is truly full of life. In the silence of our new home we have heard feathers shuffle as a bird flies overhead, and in the darkness we have seen what feels like every star. It's the desert that has guided us to a reappreciation of the simplest moments and the kind of happiness that can't be taken away.

Sara and Rich Combs
JOSHUA TREE, CALIFORNIA
@thejoshuatreehouse

Photo by Tim Melideo

Thank You

Thank you to our loving desert community who so willingly jumped in to share your knowledge, time, and ideas for this book: Geneva Karwoski, Heidi Stubler Brown, Tienlyn Jacobson, Nikko DeTranquilli, Heather Day, Aleksandra Zee, David Benhaim, Casey Goch, Kenya Knight, Taib Lotfi, Jen Mussari, Chase McBride, Anthony Angelicola, Thao Nguyen, Stella Maria Baer, Claire Wadsworth, Nikki Hill, Caris Reid, Tara Feener, Andy Gassaway, Sophia Rose, and Tim Melideo. Each one of you is an endless inspiration to us.

To our parents, who encouraged us as artists and taught us to live our dreams: Jay Combs, Colleen Combs, Angela Rossbach, and Steve Rossbach.

To Shannon Connors Fabricant, our editor, for your trust, support, and honest feedback. To Ashley Todd, the designer of this book, for seamlessly integrating our photos and stories.

And to you, as a reader…thank you for taking the time to read these words. We're beyond grateful for your support. If you find yourself in Joshua Tree, say hello! (You can find us on Instagram, we're @thejoshuatreehouse.)

Index